Culture

John Middleton

- ■ Fast track route to mastering culture and culture change

- ■ Covers the key areas of culture, from how culture evolves and why different companies have different cultures to cultural diagnosis and implementing successful change

- ■ Examples and lessons from some of the world's most successful businesses, including Amazon.com, EDS, Honda and Nissan, and ideas from the smartest thinkers, including Edgar Schein, Charles Handy, Geert Hofstede and Gareth Morgan

- ■ Includes a glossary of key concepts and a comprehensive resources guide

ORGANIZATIONS

07.04

≫EXPRESS EXEC.COM≪
essential management thinking at your fingertips

The right of John Middleton to be identified as the author of this work has been asserted in accordance with the Copyright, Designs and Patents Act 1988

First published 2002 by
Capstone Publishing (a Wiley company)
8 Newtec Place
Magdalen Road
Oxford OX4 1RE
United Kingdom
http://www.capstoneideas.com

CIP catalogue records for this book are available from the British Library and the US Library of Congress

ISBN 1-84112-216-5

FSC
Mixed Sources
Product group from well-managed
forests and other controlled sources
Cert no. SGS-COC-2953
www.fsc.org
© 1996 Forest Stewardship Council

Contents

Contents

Introduction to ExpressExec

ExpressExec is 3 million words of the latest management thinking compiled into 10 modules. Each module contains 10 individual titles forming a comprehensive resource of current business practice written by leading practitioners in their field. From brand management to balanced scorecard, ExpressExec enables you to grasp the key concepts behind each subject and implement the theory immediately. Each of the 100 titles is available in print and electronic formats.

Through the ExpressExec.com Website you will discover that you can access the complete resource in a number of ways:

» printed books or e-books;
» e-content – PDF or XML (for licensed syndication) adding value to an intranet or Internet site;
» a corporate e-learning/knowledge management solution providing a cost-effective platform for developing skills and sharing knowledge within an organization;
» bespoke delivery – tailored solutions to solve your need.

Why not visit www.expressexec.com and register for free key management briefings, a monthly newsletter and interactive skills checklists. Share your ideas about ExpressExec and your thoughts about business today.

Please contact elound@wiley-capstone.co.uk for more information.

Introduction

An organization's culture shapes how people think and behave. This chapter explores the significance of organizational culture, before concluding that organizations need to be conscious of and manage the cultures in which they are embedded, or else those cultures will manage them.

What I find interesting is the number of executives who are earnestly depending on radical cultural transformation to save their job or even their company's future.

Daryl Conner, author[1]

There is a well-known aphorism that if you want to find out about water, then don't go asking a fish. Just as water quickly becomes unremarkable when you spend all your time swimming in it, so an organization's culture can often be largely invisible to the people who have worked there for any length of time.

If you want proof of this and have worked in the same place for more than a year, try tracking down somebody who has joined your company recently, say within the last three to four weeks, and ask them what they have particularly noticed, or what has struck them as unusual about the way things are done in your company. What they highlight may well be aspects of your company's culture – cultural indicators if you like – that you have ceased to notice or come to take for granted.

Does this matter? Why should you or your company be interested in knowing more about culture? Here are four reasons why culture matters.

» Culture is not just a theoretical issue. To fully understand an organization, and to be able to manage it effectively on a day-to-day basis, you have to have an appreciation of its culture.
» Culture may be about "soft" subjects like emotion, organizational history, and collective beliefs, but those emotions and beliefs explicitly shape behavior in the real world. Culture helps us understand how behavior is created, embedded, developed, manipulated, managed, and changed.
» If a company wants to maximize its ability to attain its strategic objectives, it must understand if the prevailing culture supports and drives the actions necessary to achieve its strategic goals.
» If your competitive environment is changing fast, your organizational culture may also need to change.

For most of us, culture is something that we experience indirectly as the "atmosphere" or "climate" of the place in which we work. As such, it is often described as "the way we do things around here." This may be a common sense definition of culture, but it oversimplifies the subject and misses powerful underlying concepts and processes. We will look at a number of these in later sections.

For now, though, there is a critical and unarguable point to make about culture. It may be perceived by hard-nosed managers as a "soft" namby-pamby subject but it shouldn't be ignored for one simple reason: organizations develop cultures whether they try to or not.

This being so, there is a stark bottom line for organizations. To quote MIT Professor Edgar Schein, if organizations do not become conscious of the cultures in which they are embedded, "those cultures will manage them."[2]

The overriding purpose of this book is to give you the tools, techniques and insights you'll need to ensure that you can understand and manage your organization's culture and that you don't become its victim.

Let's make a start.

NOTES

1. Conner, D. (1993) *Managing at the Speed of Change*. Villard Books, New York.
2. Schein, E. (1992) *Organizational Culture and Leadership*. Jossey Bass, San Francisco.

Definition of Terms

Although culture is most commonly defined as "the way we do things around here," there are many definitions that we can draw on to illuminate and deepen our understanding of the concept. This chapter discusses a number of definitions by various theorists and practitioners, before going on to examine how subcultures form.

» Defining culture
» Defining subculture
» How subcultures differ
» Understanding culture is not enough
» Key learning points

"Strong cultures are like the wind. Invisible, but you know when they blow and everyone feels the same force, from the same direction."

Andy Law, chairman, St Luke's advertising agency[1]

CULTURE

There are any number of definitions that we can draw on to illuminate and deepen our understanding of the concept of culture. Depending on where you look and who you listen to, organizational culture may be defined as any of the following.

» A set of norms that create powerful precedents for acceptable behavior within the organization.
» Unwritten "rules of the road" that create expectations in an organization around acceptable risk, change orientation, creativity and innovation, group versus individual effort, customer orientation, extra effort, and more.
» A powerful force that can provide an engine to achieve market success or an anchor pulling the organization down towards failure.
» The "operating system" of the organization.
» The unique whole, the heart and soul, that determines how a group of people will behave.
» Collective beliefs that in turn shape behavior.
» The personality of the organization.
» The collective programming of the organizational mind which distinguishes the members of one human group from another.

More formally, organizational culture has been described by Geert Hofstede, one of the leading academics in the field of cultural studies, as "patterns of shared values and beliefs that over time produce behavioral norms adopted in solving problems." Elsewhere, he has defined culture as "the collective programming of the mind which distinguishes the members of one human group from another." He emphasizes that culture is not a property of the individuals, but of groups. Moreover, claims Hofstede, it is "holistic, historically determined, socially constructed and difficult to change."

Gareth Morgan, best-selling author and distinguished research professor at York University in Toronto, takes a much broader view of culture when he writes:

"What is this phenomenon we call culture? The word has been derived metaphorically from the idea of cultivation, the process of tilling and developing land. When we talk about culture, we are typically referring to the pattern of development reflected in a society's system of knowledge, ideology, values, laws, and day-to-day ritual ... Nowadays, however, the concept of culture ... [is] used more generally to signify that different groups of people have different ways of life."[2]

But perhaps the most widely used definition of organizational culture is offered by Edgar Schein, a professor at MIT who is considered one of the "founders" of organizational psychology. Schein proposes that culture can be formally defined as:

"... a pattern of shared basic assumptions that the group learned as it solved its problems of external adaptation and internal integration, that has worked well enough to be considered valid and, therefore, to be taught to new members as the correct way to perceive, think, and feel in relation to those problems."[3]

Schein's definition brings together many of the ideas and concepts expressed in that earlier list of definitions, but putting particular emphasis on shared, taken-for-granted basic assumptions held by the member of the group or organization.

Andy Law, chairman of St Luke's advertising agency, has a hands-on view of culture:[4]

"I like how Ralph Stacey defined company cultures in his excellent book *Managing the Unknowable*:[5] 'Culture is a set of beliefs or assumptions that a group of people share concerning how to see things, how to interpret events, what it is valid to question, what answers are acceptable, how to behave toward others, and how to do things. The culture of a group of people develops as they associate with each other. The most important parts of it are unconscious, and they cannot be imposed from outside, even by top management.'

"This is 'proper culture' for me, because it is honest in what it describes and practical in how it affects a company. Personally I fear cultures that will not change, have to be constantly articulated, or which cannot thrive invisibly and instructively in the hearts and minds of every employee.

"Stacey's culture is based on beliefs or assumptions that you all share. But not all types of businesses can be bothered with beliefs or assumptions unless they belong to the boss. 'Stop pussyfooting around and give me the sales data. I didn't get where I am today by believing in beliefs and assumptions,' the fictional CJ, head of Sunshine Desserts, might say. In fact the pursuit of the bottom line not only drives culture into a corner, it also dangerously and dismissively reconfigures it as niceynicey, soft stuff to 'keep the troops happy.' "

SUBCULTURES

Many companies have a strong dominant culture that is pervasive throughout the organization, across business units and regions. An organization of this type is said to possess a high level of *cultural integration*.

Very often, however, the culture in large organizations is not pervasive, singular, or uniform. In these organizations, there is not one single culture but a collection of *subcultures*. Subcultures may share certain characteristics, norms, values, and beliefs or be totally different. These subcultures can function co-operatively or be in conflict with each other.

Subcultures can differ in a number of ways. The most important areas of differentiation are outlined below.

» *Differentiation by functional/occupational activity*: Some subcultures are a product of the different functions carried out within the organization. The Production Department hires people from a manufacturing production, the Finance Department hires professionally qualified accountants, the Marketing Department hires marketing specialists, and so on. Each specialist career area has its own values, norms, preferred way of working. Each one also has its own set of language and concepts which will be readily understood by other members of the profession, but which will tend to exclude people from other backgrounds.

» *Differentiation by geographical decentralization*: For multinational companies, each location will draw on national cultural characteristics. The same is true to a degree for national companies with regional offices.

» *Differentiation by product, market, or technology*: A company selling professional quality hi-fi to a select market of audiophiles will have a different style and approach to a high street pile-it-high-sell-it-cheap outlet selling to the general public.

» *Differentiation by divisionalization*: An organization that has subdivided into divisions will find that those different divisions will often have different cultural characteristics. This will in part reflect the level to which the company has decentralized activity, but will also reflect the personality and style of those individuals heading up the individual divisions.

» *Differentiation by hierarchical level*: To co-ordinate the efforts of large numbers of people, most organizations will create hierarchical layers. Almost inevitably, and no matter how stripped down the hierarchy, "top management" will have a different culture to "middle management" who in turn will regard themselves as distinct from "the workers."

» *Differentiation by mergers and acquisitions*: Any merger involves a coming together of two separate cultures, no matter how closely matched the individual parties might appear to be. Each will have its own history, leadership style, set of assumptions about how business should be conducted, geographical base etc. and as a result there will be a host of cultural issues arising. Similar factors affect an acquisition. In fact, similar principles apply to joint ventures, strategic alliances, or multi-organizational units.

DEFINITIONS ARE USEFUL BUT HAVE THEIR LIMITS

No matter what our role in organizations, we all need to understand what culture is and how it both reflects and shapes organizational behavior. But it is particularly crucial for organizational leaders to be conscious of the culture. As Edgar Schein puts it: "Cultural understanding is desirable for all of us, but it is essential to leaders if they are to lead."[6]

But it is not enough for leaders to have an understanding of what culture is. Here is Schein again: "A formal definition of organizational culture can tell us what culture is, but it does not tell us what cultural assumptions are about, why they form in the first place, and more important, why they survive. To understand the content and dynamics of culture, we must develop a model of how basic assumptions arise and why they persist. We need such a model because ultimately culture covers all aspects of group life."[7]

It is to this more developed appreciation of where culture comes from and how it develops that we now turn our attention in Chapter 3.

KEY LEARNING POINTS

There are many definitions of culture. One of the most widely used is by Edgar Schein, who defined culture as "... a pattern of shared basic assumptions that the group learned as it solved its problems of external adaptation and internal integration, that has worked well enough to be considered valid and, therefore, to be taught to new members as the correct way to perceive, think, and feel in relation to those problems."

Subcultures evolve when an organization's culture is not pervasive, singular, or uniform.

NOTES

1 Law, A. (1998) *Open Minds*. Orion, London.

2 Morgan, G. (1986) *Images of Organization*. Sage, Newbury Park, California.

3 Schein, E. (1992) *Organizational Culture and Leadership*. Jossey Bass, San Francisco.

4 Law, A. (1998) *Open Minds*. Orion, London.

5 Stacey, R. (1993) *Managing the Unknowable*. Jossey Bass, San Francisco.

6 Schein, E. (1992) *Organizational Culture and Leadership*. Jossey Bass, San Francisco.

7 ibid.

Evolution

As long as there have been organizations, there have been organizational cultures. As a concept, however, management theorists have only been writing about culture for around 20 years. Edgar Schein writes about three levels of organizational culture – artifacts, espoused values and underlying assumptions.

» A brief history of culture
» The components of culture
» Three levels of culture
» Where are we now?
» Key learning points

"The drive for culture change derives from the need to solve organizational problems. It is only when cultural assumptions get in the way that the issue of culture change arises."

Edgar Schein[1]

A BRIEF HISTORY OF CULTURE

Edgar Schein, writing in 1992, had this to say about the history of organizational culture as a concept:

"Culture as a concept has had a long and checkered history. It has been used by the lay person as a word to indicate sophistication, as when we say that someone is very 'cultured'. It has been used by anthropologists to refer to the customs and rituals that societies develop over the course of their history. In the last decade or so it has been used by some organizational researchers and managers to indicate the climate and practices that organizations develop around their handling of people or to refer to the espoused values and credo of an organization."[2]

So, going by Schein's estimation, the notion of "organizational culture" has not been around all that long, perhaps only since the early 1980s. Even at that time, there were at best a handful of organizations that were attempting to address performance issues by shifting some aspect of their cultures. Most companies simply did not recognize the concept.

That said, for as long as organizations have existed, they have had all the features of what has come to be called culture. So if we accept the conventional wisdom that the roots of modern-day organizations can be traced back to 2000-year-old models of Chinese military hierarchy, then organizational cultures have been around for just as long. The only thing missing has been the terminology of organizational cultural studies.

What has happened over the past 20 years has been a process of successive management thinkers and practitioners retro-fitting organizational cultural models and terminology to bygone management research.

As an example, when Henri Fayol (1841–1925), a mining engineer and manager by profession, defined the nature and working patterns of the twentieth-century organization in his book, *General and Industrial Management*, published in 1916, he laid down what he called 14 principles of management.

HENRY FAYOL'S 14 PRINCIPLES OF MANAGEMENT

1 *Division of work*: Tasks should be divided up with employees specializing in a limited set of tasks so that expertise is developed and productivity increased.

2 *Authority and responsibility*: Authority is the right to give orders and entails enforcing them with rewards and penalties; authority should be matched with corresponding responsibility.

3 *Discipline*: Discipline is essential for the smooth running of business and is dependent on good leadership, clear and fair arguments, and the judicious application of penalties.

4 *Unity of command*: For any action whatsoever, an employee should receive orders from one superior only; otherwise authority, discipline, order, and stability are threatened.

5 *Unity of direction*: A group of activities concerned with a single objective should be co-ordinated by a single plan under one head.

6 *Subordination of individual interest to general interest*: Individual or group goals must not be allowed to override those of the business.

7 *Remuneration of personnel*: This may be achieved by various methods but it should be fair, encourage effort, and not lead to overpayment.

8 *Centralization*: The extent to which orders should be issued only from the top of the organization is a problem which should take into account its characteristics, such as size and the capabilities of the personnel.

9 *Scalar chain (line of authority)*: Communications should normally flow up and down the line of authority, running from the top to the bottom of the organization, but sideways

communication between those of equivalent rank in different departments can be desirable so long as superiors are kept informed.

10 *Order*: Both materials and personnel must always be in their proper place; people must be suited to their posts so there must be careful organization of work and selection of personnel.

11 *Equity*: Personnel must be treated with kindness and justice.

12 *Stability of tenure of personnel*: Rapid turnover of personnel should be avoided because of the time required for the development of expertise.

13 *Initiative*: All employees should be encouraged to exercise initiative within limits imposed by the requirements of authority and discipline.

14 *Esprit de corps*: Efforts must he made to promote harmony within the organization and prevent dissension and divisiveness.

In defining the core principles governing how organizations worked and the contribution of management to that process, he in effect laid down a blueprint for a particular cultural model, a model that modern-day cultural theorists would called a Role Culture (for more information on Role Cultures, see Chapter 6).

Similarly, when Frederick W Taylor, "the father of scientific management" and arguably the world's first management consultant, took his ideas about how organizations could be most efficiently managed into the workplace, he set the pattern for industrial working practice worldwide. His "five simple principles" implicitly pointed the twentieth-century organization towards the Role Culture model – around 70 years before the term was coined.

SCIENTIFIC MANAGEMENT: TAYLOR'S FIVE SIMPLE PRINCIPLES

1 Shift all responsibility for the organization of work from the worker to the manager; managers should do all the thinking

relating to the planning and design of work, leaving the workers with the task of implementation.

2 Use scientific methods to determine the most efficient way of doing work; assign the worker's task accordingly, specifying the precise way in which the work is to be done.

3 Select the best person to perform the job thus designed.

4 Train the worker to do the work efficiently.

5 Monitor worker performance to ensure that appropriate work procedures are followed and that appropriate results are achieved.

Because the industrialists of the early decades of the twentieth century followed Taylor's lead and put the emphasis on efficiency, it was some years before any significant attention was paid to the needs and motivations of that other major factor involved in the work process – the workers. One of the early pioneers of a view that actually people were central to the world of business was Mary Parker Follett (1868–1933). Although she has achieved an almost legendary status since her death, her views were largely ignored at the time by the business world.

However, the seeds were sown, and a number of people setting up businesses in the 1930s – people like Bill Hewlett and Dave Packard, for instance – began to realize that the nature of the relationship between a company and its workforce impacted explicitly on the quality of contribution that individuals made. Treat people with respect and bear their needs and interests in mind, and they typically make a better contribution. Treat them as production fodder, and they park their brains outside before walking through the gates of the company and into work.

This slowly growing realization on the part of some organizations that extracting the optimal performance out of people required a more subtle understanding of the human heart and mind led to the creation of companies with a very different look and feel to them compared to the efficiency-obsessed Taylorist companies against which they were a reaction.

Although these differences were clearly observable, the world of management theorists described these differences in terms of various organizational structures and a range of behavioral and motivational models like Douglas McGregor's Theory X and Theory Y.

It has only been over the past 20 years or so that corporate culture has become a hot topic in business books and journals, and consequently – or at least in tandem with this – the number of organizations attempting some form of explicit culture change has steadily increased.

There is, however, a huge problem facing business leaders wishing to change the culture of their organizations. And that is the very idea of trying to "change the culture." Ever since the concept of organizational culture was broached as an important element in understanding organizations, some companies have been engaged in a meaningless and wholly inappropriate search for the "right kind" of culture, and have been hiring consultants to help them foster or install those cultures.

It is as though these organizations saw culture as some kind of tangible and malleable entity that lurks in the corridors, and which is somehow distinct from the fabric of the business. Organizations thought that if only they could trade in their current culture for a spanking new model, probably imported directly from another organization that they admire, everything would be alright.

This simplistic, optimistic view of culture began to fade around ten years ago as a growing band of theorists and practitioners, led by Edgar Schein, blew away any ideas that culture was a simple and self-contained concept. In its stead came a view of culture as a complex entity that is perpetuated and transmitted by a whole host of factors. These include:

» the underlying philosophy and values of the organization;
» organizational systems and procedures;
» recruitment, performance, and promotion systems;
» the organization's design and structure;
» the behavior modeled by management;
» the stories, legends, and myths about key people and events; and
» how the organization is designed and structured.

A 1992 study by Kotter and Heskett[3] supported Schein's view that changing an organization's culture is messy, complicated business. Their study also indicated that culture change becomes tougher as organizations become more established and successful. The very bases for a company's earlier success can be hindrances to changes needed under new and different scenarios from those which existed previously.

As a means of trying to give some shape and structure to thinking about organizational culture, Schein has suggested that the components of culture can be sub-divided into three levels (see Fig. 3.1).[4]

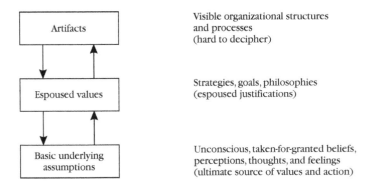

Fig. 3.1   Edgar Schein's three levels of culture.

At the surface, we have the level of *artifacts*, which includes everything we might see, hear, or feel when we come across a new organization. Artifacts would include the physical environment (is the working environment open plan or does it consist of rabbit warrens of individual offices, for example); all visible behaviors; the way people dress; rituals and ceremonies; published documents; the technology used; and so on.

An outsider or a new starter can often spot these artifacts easily upon entering an organization. For employees who have been around the organization for a while, these artifacts have often become part of the background. This level of culture, says Schein, is easy to see but often difficult to decipher.

The second level is that of *espoused values*. This is what an organization says it believes. Sometimes this will be manifest in the artifacts of the organization e.g. an espoused value that open communication is important may show itself in the form of regular briefings for employees, or the way an office is laid out, or in the content of the corporate mission statement. Sometimes, however, these values will be espoused but not enacted. These moments of discrepancy between what an organizations says it believes and what it does in practice are in themselves highly indicative of the type of organizational culture that prevails.

The third level that Schein identifies reflects the *basic underlying assumptions* that have become so taken for granted that people in the organization would find it inconceivable to base their behavior on anything else. For example, a company's deeply held belief that the customer should always be treated with respect would render it almost impossible that organizational employees would set out to deliberately rip off customers. These deeply held assumptions are rarely articulated and even more rarely are they questioned unless some form of organizational crisis forces their re-examination. So any form of culture change that provokes this would provoke extreme anxiety in most employees.

The central issue for leaders has become how to get at the deeper levels of a culture, how to assess the continuing validity of the assumptions currently held, and how to deal with the concerns that are unleashed when those assumptions are challenged.

WHERE ARE WE NOW?

As a field of organizational study, culture has two unusual aspects: firstly, it is a very young discipline, around a couple of decades old; and secondly, the fundamental models and principles evolved very quickly during the 1980s and early 1990s and haven't significantly changed since that time.

This second point may sound surprising given the amount of change organizations have had to contend with in recent time, and given the whole e-business phenomenon. Surely there are now some fundamentally different organizational models around? Surely technology has had a significant impact on organizations? Surely the demise of the "job for life" has impacted on organizational life?

All of these points are valid – organizations do change and evolve, and so do individuals' expectations of organizational life. However, the tools of cultural analysis developed around 10–15 years ago have remained valid. In some cases, those tools may have evolved a bit, but there has been no quantum leap or paradigm shift in the field of cultural studies since then.

The main stumbling block for many organizations is that they retain to this day a naïve and simplistic view of their culture and how it can be changed. But the issue is less about the existence of appropriate insights about managing cultural challenges, and more about the willingness of many organizations to give culture the attention it deserves and the long-term commitment it requires to make a substantial and positive difference.

KEY LEARNING POINTS

Although the notion of "culture" has been around for hundreds of years, the concept of "organizational culture" is much more recent, probably dating back to the early 1980s.

This simplistic, optimistic view of culture began to fade around ten years ago as a growing band of theorists and practitioners, led by Edgar Schein, blew away any ideas that culture was a simple and self-contained concept.

NOTES

1 Schein, E. (1992) *Organizational Culture and Leadership*, 2nd edn. Jossey Bass, San Francisco.
2 ibid.
3 Kotter, J. & Heskett, J. (1992). *Corporate Culture and Performance*. The Free Press, New York.
4 Schein, E. (1992) *Organizational Culture and Leadership*, 2nd edn. Jossey Bass, San Francisco.

The E-Dimension

The Internet is having a significant impact on organizations and hence organizational culture. This chapter includes the following sections.

» Competition comes in all shapes and sizes
» Intangibles rule
» The local labor exchange has become a global job market
» 24/7 is the new 9-to-5
» Start-ups are built on greenfield sites
» Start-ups can recruit freely from the best on the market
» Hierarchy diminished
» Decision making becomes more collaborative and decentralized
» Internal communication – the challenge of fast growth
» Not enough talented people to go around
» More demanding customers
» Case study: Amazon.com
» Key learning points

"We thought the creation and operation of Websites was mysterious Nobel prize stuff, the province of the wild-eyed and purple-haired. Any company, old or new, that does not see this technology as important as breathing could be on its last breath."

Jack Welch, former chairman of General Electric[1]

Even if you strip away all the hype, it is difficult to escape the conclusion that we are increasingly living in a dotcom world. To date, most attention has been focused on the snazzy business models underpinning e-businesses. Less has been said about how the Internet impacts on organizations and the people who work in them.

So what has been the explicit impact? How is organizational life changing on the back of technological advancement?

One thing is clear. The impact of information technology on organizations has already been significant and can only increase over the coming years. Directly or indirectly, technology is redefining the nature of organizations and work. New computer-based systems dissolve all organizational conventions of ownership, design, manufacturing, executive style, and national identity.

Here are just a few of the ways in which technology has impacted on organizational life.

» *Competition comes in all shapes and sizes*: The competitor who devours sizeable chunks of your customer base could be a mega-corporation with huge resources and deep pockets; equally, it could be an enthusiastic twenty-something with an idea and a computer, who intuitively understands that it is now perfectly possible to become a one-person global enterprise. There is, in short, hardly a company in existence that is not vulnerable to the Internet's potential to diminish the significance of, for example, size, location, time, distance, and physical resources.

» *Intangibles rule*: When it comes to achieving business success, the traditional factors of production – land, labor, and capital – are rapidly becoming restraints rather than driving forces. Knowledge has become the central, key resource.

» *The local labor exchange has become a global job market*: Manufacturing capacity will continue to shift from Western economies to those countries with access to cheaper labor. Equally, technology is allowing more and more knowledge-based work to be shipped to the cheapest environment.

» *24/7 is the new 9-to-5*: The "working day" has no meaning in a global village where communication via electronic mail, voice mail, and facsimile transmissions can be sent or received at any time of day or night.

» *Start-ups are built on greenfield sites*: Start-ups have no cultural baggage. They can concentrate on their business objectives in the confidence that their corporate culture will be supportive. This contrasts sharply with many bricks-and-mortar companies whose e-business ventures have often caused corporate culture turmoil.

» *Start-ups can recruit freely from the best on the market*: Most bricks-and-mortar CEOs are pretty unenamored of the people that work for them and alongside them. A survey carried out in 1999 by the Institute of Directors and Development Dimensions International asked senior directors what percentage of their employees they would re-hire if they could change all their employees overnight. Half said they would re-hire between 0% and 40%. Only 7%, moreover, expressed confidence in the leadership capabilities of their peers within their organizations.

Start-ups do not face these problems, at least not in the early days. The organization is consciously designed and the people involved are handpicked. They do not, in short, suffer from what a CEO client of mine calls "inherited incompetence."

» *Hierarchy diminished*: A traditional organization is structured around two key concepts – the breakdown and management of goals and tasks through the use of hierarchy and stable employee relationships over prolonged periods of time. In start-ups, structures are more flexible and dynamic. Hierarchy has not vanished but it has been augmented by distributed lattices of interconnections.

In an interview on The Motley Fool Radio Show in April 2000, CEO Tim Koogle described the set-up at Yahoo! thus: "It's not hierarchical. We do have a structure in the company because you need a structure to have some order on things, but it's a pretty flat organization."

» *Decision making becomes more collaborative and decentralized*: In an e-business, as with more traditional businesses, the leadership team typically make all the big strategic decisions about what the company is going to do. The difference is that decision-making in e-businesses is often a more collaborative process. At Yahoo! for example, Tim Koogle has described how working in adjoining cubicles affects the leadership team's approach to decision making: "During a normal day, you'll find us hollering back and forth across the wall, bouncing around inside the cubes, grabbing each other and going off into a little conference room."

Another facet of decision making in start-ups is that companies grow too fast to be managed closely from the center. Decisions, once taken centrally, are rapidly devolved to those working in the business to determine the method and manner of implementation.

» *Internal communication – the challenge of fast growth*: This is not a problem in the early days when the start-up organization consists of a small group of highly motivated people who spend a lot of time in each other's company, and who therefore automatically keep themselves and each other in the picture. However, business growth needs to be fuelled by new blood. By definition these are people who were not part of the original set-up and therefore processes and systems need to be introduced to ensure that everybody is kept informed – it no longer happens naturally.

For start-ups, the speed of growth means that the need for more formalized communication systems can kick in very quickly. The ill-fated boo.com, for example, went from 12 or so people to over 400 in less than a year.

» *Not enough talented people to go around*: For most e-businesses, the factor that limits or enables rapid growth is their capacity to recruit and retain good people. Finding the right people to sustain rapid growth is problematic for any business at any stage of its lifecycle. For an unproven e-business start-up, particularly now that the Internet economy has lost its luster, it can be virtually impossible. Significantly, most of the consultancy fees paid by e-business start-ups to date have gone to specialist recruitment companies.

» *More demanding customers*: We are living in an age of ever more demanding customers. They want better quality, they want cheaper prices and, above all, they want it now. The bookshop owner who tells a customer that it will take two weeks to order in the book they want is seeing increasing volumes of business going to Internet sites like Amazon. Until very recently, you had physically to go to a bank to get a balance on your account; now it's available online, more or less instantly. Providing an immediate, customer-satisfying response to any request is a tough challenge for any business. But companies who wish to remain in the marketplace have only one choice – they must become a real-time business in a world of instant gratification and infinite opportunity.

AMAZON.COM: FOLLOW THE LEADER

Amazon.com have a very clear vision: it is to be "the world's most customer-centric company. The place where people come to find and discover anything they might want to buy on-line."

Underpinning that vision are six core values:

» customer obsession
» ownership
» bias for action
» frugality
» high hiring bar
» innovation.

Amazon.com is a classic example of an organization whose values have a physical embodiment in the shape of the company's founder, Jeff Bezos. His actions and behavior shape and frame the company's culture.

For example, in the early days of the company, Bezos took every opportunity to spend only the minimum necessary. On one famous occasion, he went to Home Depot and bought three wooden doors for $60, from which he fashioned three desks. The story entered Amazon folklore and is an excellent illustration of how a core value – in this case, frugality – can be reinforced by a symbolic (and, as it happens, highly practical) act. To this day, company employees, many of them millionaires from stock options, work in small, shared offices at Bezos-designed door-desks. In fact design director Helen Owen has been quoted as saying that she fully expects to have a door-desk in five years, even if Amazon flourishes.

Bezos also regularly implores his people to be customer-obsessed. "Wake up every morning terrified," he once told a meeting of company employees, "not of the competition but of our customers."

Although it was Bezos' realization in 1994 that Web usage was growing at a phenomenal rate that set the entire online retailing phenomenon in motion, it is the personal stamp that he puts on the business that more than anything has enabled it to become the world's best known and most highly regarded online book retailer.

So what then are the practical implications for companies looking to build corporate culture in an e-business environment? In their brilliant book *Culture.com*,[2] Peg C. Neuhauser, Ray Bender, and Kirk L. Stromberg offer some practical advice in the form of "ten tips."

1 *Recruiting for cultural fit*: Building and sustaining a corporate culture that fits your needs requires a critical mass of employees who are committed to the culture's core beliefs and values. It is easier to recruit people with those traits than to change their personalities, beliefs, and behaviors once they are hired. Ask questions in the interviews and listen for cultural fit: you may be hiring somebody with the right technical or professional skills but they may damage your chances of building the culture you want.

2 *Speed up your culture*: Pick a high-priority project and decide to set a firm deadline for completion that is shorter than normal. This will force people to change their thinking about time. The question "How much time will it take to complete this project?" is replaced by "How do we manage this project so we can meet the deadline with a high-quality outcome?"

3 *When changing your culture, you get one point for each action*: Changing a culture does not happen as a result of one big corporate meeting to announce the new direction and inspire the troops. Think of it this way: you get one point for each new behavior that represents the new culture. It takes many detailed actions

throughout the company to accumulate enough points to trigger a real change in the culture.

4 *Lead more, manage less*: Lead your organization or team like it is a workforce made up entirely of volunteers. This requires you to use more leadership skills and fewer management skills. A dotcom culture has informal leaders throughout the organization at all levels. The formal leaders must set the direction, inspire, and empower those informal leaders to create a fast, innovative e-business culture.

5 *Pick credible role models*: One of the best tools for building a corporate culture is to identify role models. These employees are stellar examples of the cultural traits you want to encourage (e.g., speed, risk taking, customer service, team skills). Be sure you pick people that employees respect. There must be general agreement among managers and employees that this person deserves to be honored. Mistakes in picking role models lead to cynicism about the culture.

6 *Protect the dotcom teams from the corporate immune system*: When teams are working on e-business projects or other innovative efforts, the traditional groups within the organization tend to be hostile toward those groups and their ideas. An organization has an immune system just like the human body. If it senses a new idea in its midst, it surrounds that idea like white blood cells and kills it. Teams working on these projects need strong sponsor support to protect them in the early stages. They also must keep a low profile.

7 *Increase the collective IQ of your company*: Bring people together to discuss events when they are finished and to learn collectively from your mistakes as well as your successes. Many traditional companies have a culture that encourages employees to hide mistakes for fear of retribution. A company will have a difficult time increasing its collective IQ if it cannot discuss and learn from its mistakes. Create a few heroes out of high-profile mistake-makers, to demonstrate the kind of corporate IQ you want in your company.

8 *Enhance your company's knowledge management system*: Carry out a knowledge management assessment. If you want to improve your organization's methods for managing knowledge, start by determining your current state.

9 *Plan the integration of your parallel cultures*: Temporary groups can form such strong cultures that it is difficult to disband them later. If you are setting up an Internet division or another type of separate group to do the early development work on your Internet business, plan for the group's integration into the larger company from the project's beginning. Make sure everyone knows this is a temporary structure for the early phase and make plans early about how and when this group will merge with the larger organization.

10 *Clarify each party's commitment level in alliances*: When you set up an alliance with another company, be sure you both have the same understanding of the commitment level. You may think you are entering into a full-blown partnership with flexible give and take in the way you will work together, but if the other company sees the alliance as simply a contractual relationship in which it is not obligated to do anything not spelled out in the contract, you may be headed for trouble. As the relationship progresses, make sure you stay at the same commitment level.

Neuhauser, Bender, and Stromberg believe that corporate cultures will continue to change as companies race to implement their e-business strategies, and they lay great emphasis on the importance of the two elements working in tandem. They finish their book with a sobering observation: if your business strategy and your corporate culture are pulling in two different directions, the culture will win no matter how brilliant your strategy is.

KEY LEARNING POINTS

Here are ten practical tips for companies looking to build corporate culture in an e-business environment.

1 Recruit for cultural fit.
2 Speed up your culture.
3 When changing your culture, you get one point for each action.
4 Lead more, manage less.
5 Pick credible role models.
6 Protect the dotcom teams from the corporate immune system.

7 Increase the collective IQ of your company.
8 Enhance your company's knowledge management system.
9 Plan the integration of your parallel cultures.
10 Clarify each party's commitment level in alliances.

NOTES

1 Quoted in *The Observer*, May 14, 2000.
2 Neuhauser, P.C., Bender, R. & Stromberg, K.L. (2000) *Culture.com*. John Wiley & Sons, New York.

The Global Dimension

Although it is fashionable to talk of the MacDonaldization of society, many countries are displaying a distinct resistance to cultural homogenization. This chapter explores how cultures vary between countries.

- » Geert Hofstede's Dimensions of cultural variability
- » Globalization does not equate to homogenization
- » Honda: glocalization in action

"Management in this age of assumed globalization is an area where cultural insight is essential, and often amazingly lacking among senior decision-makers. As you may remember, a few years ago our national airline KLM announced a Strategic Alliance with Alitalia. When asked by a journalist if he did not expect cultural problems, the President of KLM was recorded as saying: 'No I don't, because Dutch people like Italian food and Italians like Dutch football-players.' To me and to a number of others, at the moment a Chief Executive made such a statement, the alliance was already doomed – and as you know it failed."

Geert Hofstede, Emeritus Professor of Organizational Anthropology and International Management at Maastricht University in the Netherlands[1]

"As the tragic record of Western economic advisers in post-Soviet Russia shows, it may be difficult for intelligent and well-intentioned academics and consultants even to grasp what is happening in environments so different from their own, and shaped by such different histories and cultures. Indeed, in a world filled with such inequalities, to live in the favored regions is to be virtually cut off from the experience, let alone the reactions, of people outside those regions. It takes an enormous effort of the imagination, as well as a great deal of knowledge, to break out of our comfortable, protected, and self-absorbed enclaves and enter an uncomfortable and unprotected larger world inhabited by the majority of the human species."

Eric Hobsbawm, historian and author[2]

Most commentators seem to take the view that globalization is having a direct and, to a degree, homogenizing impact on countries, both economically and politically.

There are also those who argue that what we're experiencing is not just the globalization, but rather the Americanization, of the world economy, with a global consumer culture being spread by companies like McDonald's and Coca-Cola. Less visibly, the global market for all of the main professional services – auditing, accounting, consulting, investment banking – are dominated by American companies.

Before we get too carried away, let's bear in mind that there are those who remain skeptical about the extent of the impact of globalization. Francis Fukuyama, author and former deputy director of the US State Department's policy planning staff, for one, has expressed his doubts:

> "I think that in many respects, globalization is still superficial. Although there is a great deal of talk about it currently, the underlying truth is that the global economy is still limited. It seems to me that the real layer of globalization is restricted to the capital markets. In most other areas, institutions remain intensely local . . . Trade, for example, is still predominantly regional."[3]

Many countries are displaying a distinct resistance to cultural homogenization. This is important when considering the roots of economic behavior and the determinants of national economic success, because culture is of critical importance to everyday economic life. Taking this premise a step further, if a national culture has some kind of impact on national economic behavior, what is at the heart of national culture?

Every time we visit a foreign country, we are reminded how different other places can look, sound, smell, and taste compared to "back home." What people eat and drink for breakfast, the times that the shops are open for business, the stories featured on the front page of newspapers – these are just a few of hundreds of examples of how what is normal and taken for granted in one country can be at odds with the practices and habits of other countries. It would be surprising if these differences didn't extend to the workplace and, sure enough, they do.

Just ask Geert Hofstede, currently Emeritus Professor of Organizational Anthropology and International Management at Maastricht University in the Netherlands. He is best known for his work on the differences between national cultures and their approach to work.

His key model depicts four aspects of cultural variability between countries, generally referred to as Hofstede's Dimensions.[4] He arrived at these elements following a study which collected survey data from a sample size of 116,000 people who worked for a multinational corporation.

His four key elements, or "dimensions," of culture are as follows:

» *Power distance*: This is a measure of the inequality between bosses and inferiors, and the extent to which this is accepted.
» *Uncertainty avoidance*: This dimension looks at the degree to which people are comfortable with ambiguous situations, and can tolerate uncertainty.
» *Individualism vs. collectivism*: This is about the degree to which people think in terms of "I" versus "we," and whether ties between individuals are loose or people are part of cohesive groups throughout their lives.
» *Masculinity vs. femininity*: Also known as *achievement vs. relationship-orientation*; cultures that are high on masculinity rate achievement and success more than they do caring for others and the quality of life.

Some time later, Hofstede added a fifth dimension – *Confucian dynamism* – which assesses the extent to which different cultures have a long or short term orientation. He found that people from the same country were likely to cluster around similar points on the scale for the various characteristics, but that these points varied significantly from nationality to nationality.

YOU GOT TO HAVE TRUST

Francis Fukuyama believes that the level of trust present in a society is the key, performance-determining aspect of national culture and that only those societies with a high degree of social trust will be able to create the flexible, large scale business organizations that are needed to compete in the new global economy.

In his book *Trust: the Social Virtues and the Creation of Prosperity*,[5] Fukuyama describes three types of trust. The first is based on the family, the second revolves around voluntary associations beyond the family, and the third concerns the state. Each of the three categories has a corresponding organizational form; the family business, the professionally managed corporation and the state-owned enterprise, respectively.

In countries where family ties are strong (and trust of those outside the family correspondingly weak), people tend to look to the state to create the large professionally managed corporations. Societies with high levels of trust seem to be capable of creating large economic organizations without state support. Fukuyama cites China, South Korea, Italy, and France as low trust societies with a strong role for the family and weak associations outside the family group. In contrast, he claims, Japan, the United States, and Germany are high trust societies with strong and plentiful associations beyond the family.

Fons Trompenaars, another Dutch academic in the area of cross-cultural understanding, undertook research to identify national cultural differences which manifest themselves within corporate cultures. Like Hofstede, he identified a number of dimensions in which cultures can differ. These are set out below, and in each case include a quote from Trompenaars[6] to explain the focus of the dimension.

» *Universalism vs. pluralism* (a focus on rules and procedures or relationships): "The universalist approach is roughly: 'What is good and right can be defined and always applies.' In particularist cultures far greater attention is given to the obligations of relationships and unique circumstances. For example, instead of assuming that the one good way must always be followed, the particularist reasoning is that friendship has special obligations and hence may come first. Less attention is given to abstract societal codes."
» *Individualism vs. communitarianism* (me or the group): "The individualist society, with its respect for individual opinions, will frequently ask for a vote to get all noses pointing in the same direction. The drawback to this is that within a short time they are likely to have reverted to their original orientation. The collectivist society will intuitively refrain from voting because this will not show respect to the individuals who are against the majority decision. It prefers to deliberate until consensus is reached. The final result takes longer to achieve, but will be much more stable. In individualistic societies there is frequently disparity between decision and implementation."

» *Specific vs. diffuse* (superficial or deep relationships; whether bits of life are kept apart or brought together): "In the case of one American company trying to win a contract with a South American customer, disregard for the importance of the relationship lost the deal. The American company made a slick, well-thought-out presentation which it thought clearly demonstrated its superior product and lower price. Its Swedish competitor took a week to get to know the customer. For five days the Swedish spoke about everything except the product. On the last day the product was introduced. Though somewhat less attractive and slightly higher priced, the diffuse involvement of the Swedish company got the order."

» *Neutrality vs. affectivity* (conceal or show emotions): "In North America and north-west Europe business relationships are typically instrumental and all about achieving objectives. The brain checks emotions because these are believed to confuse the issues . . . But further south and in many other cultures, business is a human affair and the whole gamut of emotions deemed appropriate. Loud laughter, banging your fist on the table or leaving a conference room in anger during a negotiation is all part of business."

» *Inner-directed vs. outer-directed* (the environment around): "Cultures vary in their approaches to the given environment, between belief that it can be controlled by the individual and belief that the individual must respond to external circumstances. We should not, however, make the error of assuming that inner-direction and outer-direction are exclusive options. All cultures necessarily take some notice of what is inside or outside. To fail to do so would lead inner-directed cultures into a headlong rush to disaster, while outer-directed cultures would try to please everyone and dissipate their energies by over-compliance."

» *Achieved status vs. ascribed status* (from who you are or what you do): "In an achievement culture, the first question is likely to be 'What did you study?', while in a more ascriptive culture the question will more likely be 'Where did you study?' Only if it was a lousy university or one they do not recognize will ascriptive people ask what you studied, and that will be to enable you to save face."

» *Sequential time vs. synchronic time* (one after another or all at once): "In certain cultures like the American, Swedish and Dutch, time is perceived as passing in a straight line, a sequence of disparate events. Other cultures think of time more as moving in a circle, the past and the present together with future possibilities.''

Between them, Hofstede and Trompenaars dispel the idea that there is only one globally accepted way to manage a business. Every country has its own preferred set of patterns and practices. Given these differences, one of the greatest challenges for any organization operating in international markets is to identify and manage how it varies the way it does business in other countries.

Even McDonald's, so often held up as an example of cultural imperialism, has embraced the concept of ''glocalization,'' the idea that products or services can be created for the global market, but need to be customized to suit the local culture. A study of McDonald's restaurants conducted by James Watson,[7] an anthropologist at Harvard University, found that McDonald's, despite its reputation for being a standardized American juggernaut plowing over everything like a steamroller, adapts to local conditions and changes its behavior considerably from country to country.

For example, Watson says that in North America and Europe there is an implicit contract between McDonald's and its customers: the company provides inexpensive, clean food, and the customer eats it and goes quickly. This does not work in East Asia, where one key group of customers are high school students who go to McDonald's after school, spending anything up to three hours there, eating and doing their homework before going home. The menu also varies somewhat between countries.

If even McDonald's has to localize, how much more other companies?

So globalization does not equate to homogenization. As consumers seek more choice, companies that find themselves stretched to deliver what customers want will fall prey to others that can accommodate their needs. Perhaps the overriding impact of globalization on business culture is that it intensifies the need for companies to strive for excellence. Jack Welch, as ever, states it succinctly:[8] ''The winning companies in the global competition will be those companies that can put together the best of research, engineering, design, manufacturing, distribution – wherever they can get it, anywhere in the world – and the best of each of these will not come from one country or from one continent."

HONDA: GLOCALIZATION IN ACTION

Honda began life in 1946 as a small motorcycle manufacturer and is now a business that sells annually around 11 million products worldwide, including automobiles, motorcycles, and power products. The company has seen record-setting sales in the last three years, but still manages to retain the qualities of a small company.

Unlike other global businesses that see size as the key to survival, Honda is determined to maintain the qualities of a small company that is close to its customers. The company has the ability to produce a worthwhile product with the speed, flexibility, and efficiency of a small company, and combines this with the essential elements of a large company – global reach and technological strength. This approach is reflected in Honda's declared mission to "continue to develop and build products in local markets around the world to create value for all of our customers."

In the early 1990s, Honda created five divisions to correspond with different regions of the world: North America, Europe/Middle East/Africa, South America, Asia/Oceania and Japan. Within this set-up, decision-making responsibility for sales, manufacturing, and research were devolved to each region. Products that best served the region were pushed to the forefront of that area's development and manufacturing process.

For example, when Honda launched its Accord model in 1998, the company was convinced that a single version of the car would not meet the needs of customers in every market in the world. So Honda's Research and Development group in Japan set out to create a flexible template for the car. Regional R&D groups in the United States and Europe adapted the template to best fit their respective customer's needs. Worldwide co-operation among the five regions produced a cost-effective and locally tailored solution for each region.

So what is Honda's global strategy? It's simple – put cost-effective plants in areas that best meet the needs of local customers. This "glocalization" strategy benefits local customers as well as their communities. Production is started small and is expanded as local demand increases. This thinking has helped Honda establish more than 100 factories in 33 countries, and is an approach that allows the company to achieve efficiency and profitability, even at low production volumes.

KEY LEARNING POINTS

Geert Hofstede has a model that depicts four aspects of cultural variability between countries, generally referred to as Hofstede's Dimensions. The four key elements, or "dimensions", of culture are: Power distance; Uncertainty avoidance; Individualism vs. collectivism; and Masculinity vs. femininity.

Fons Trompenaars, another Dutch academic, emphasizes: Universalism vs. pluralism (a focus on rules and procedures or relationships); Individualism vs. communitarianism (me or the group); Specific vs. diffuse (superficial or deep relationships; whether bits of life are kept apart or brought together); Neutrality vs. affectivity (conceal or show emotions); Inner-directed vs. outer-directed (the environment around); Achieved status vs. ascribed status (from who you are or what you do); and Sequential time vs. synchronic time (one after another or all at once).

NOTES

1 Extract from Geert Hofstede's acceptance speech on being awarded an Honorary Doctorate in Business Administration at Nyenrode University, Monday September 3, 2001.
2 Hobsbawm, E. (2000) *The New Century*. Little Brown, New York.
3 Francis Fukuyama, speaking at a Merrill Lynch Forum in 1998, www.ml.com/woml/forum/global.htm
4 These dimensions were first reported in Hofstede, G. (1980) *Culture's Consequences: international differences in work-related values*. Sage.

5 Fukuyama, F. (2000) *Trust: the Social Virtues and the Creation of Prosperity*. Hamish Hamilton, London.

6 Trompenaars, F. (1993) *Riding the Waves of Culture*. Nicholas Brealey, London.

7 Watson, J. (1998) *Golden Arches East*. Stanford University Press, Stanford, California.

8 Quoted in Ashkenas, R., Ulrich, D., Jick, T. & Kerr, S. (1996) *The Boundaryless Organization: Breaking the Chains of Organizational Structure*. Jossey Bass, San Francisco.

The State of the Art

» Four classifications of culture
» Six factors which influence how a culture develops
» Key issues in culture
» Key learning points

"If you work in a company with more than four employees that's been in business for more than two months, you have an organizational or company culture."

Russ Giles[1]

"The only prediction that will hold true is that no predictions will hold true."

Charles Handy[2]

The business airwaves are overwhelmed by books, articles, conferences, and videos exhorting the modern manager to take on board the latest big ideas: the application of complexity theory to business; lessons behind the rise and fall of the dotcoms; the ripped up psychological contract between organization and individual; the balanced scorecard; managing in a downturn; the end of loyalty; the return of loyalty; emotional intelligence; the narcissistic leader; and so on. Some may have long-lasting value for the discerning manager; others will almost certainly turn out to be dead ends.

In this section, we will explore a handful of the emergent ideas and concepts relating to organizational culture that are currently clamoring for managerial attention. Hopefully, they will provoke your thinking. Reflect on them, discuss them with colleagues, and beyond that, trust your own judgement.

TYPOLOGIES OF ORGANIZATIONAL CULTURE

Different organizations have different cultures. We know instinctively that a library has a different set of operating principles to a street market. To help us get to grips with and understand these different organizational cultures, we can use various models and frameworks that can provide a "shortcut" to providing that understanding.

Defining "models or frameworks" enable us to understand what the phenomenon is, discuss it with others, and identify what we might do to translate the model or parts of it into reality. Writer, management guru, and social philosopher Charles Handy has drawn on the work of Roger Harrison to suggest that there are four basic cultural types that operate to a greater or lesser extent in western organizations.[3]

The four classifications are:

1 Power Cultures
2 Role Cultures
3 Task Cultures
4 Person Cultures.

Let's examine each in turn.

1. Power Culture

» *Overview*: This model is like a web with a ruling spider. Those in the web are dependent on a central power source. There may be a specialist or functional structure but central control is exercised largely through appointing loyal key individuals and interventionist behavior from the center. For people working there, it can be a case of "Conform or Go!"

» *How it works*: This culture tends to rely on a central figure for its strength, and has lines of communication which not only radiate out from this center but also link sideways across the organization. The dominant influence of the center results in a structure that is able to move quickly and respond to change and outside threats. This ability is gained not by formal methods but by the selection of like-minded individuals who in key positions are able to guess what the chief executive would do and act in accordance with their presumed wishes.

» *Advantages*: Organizations like this are strong, decisive, and dynamic, and are able to react quickly to external demands.

» *Drawbacks*:
  » Power cultures can suffer from staff disaffection. People in the middle layers may feel they have no scope for initiative.
  » The constant need to refer to the center may create dysfunctional competition and jostling for the support of the boss.
  » The organization is dependent on the ability and judgement of the central power – if it is weak then the organization will struggle.

» *Where you'll find it*: This culture is often found in small entrepreneurial organizations and in larger companies with a strong charismatic leader.

2. Role Culture

» *Overview*: Bureaucratic in outlook, a role culture is controlled by procedures, role descriptions, and clearly delegated authority. Co-ordination occurs at the top. Because it is a culture that values predictability and consistency, it is often slow to make changes.

» *How it works*: Perhaps the most readily recognized and common of all the cultural types, the Role Culture is based around defined jobs, roles, and procedures rather than personalities. It is epitomized by the traditional hierarchical structure and works by logic and ratio-nality. The organization is delineated with clearly defined roles – the accounts department, the sales department etc. Work is co-ordinated from the top. Employees are appointed into roles based on their ability to carry out the functions – satisfactory performance of role. Performance over and above role is not expected and may disrupt.

» *Advantages*: The strengths of the Role Culture are in its predictability and stability.

Works very well when economies of scale are more important than flexibility, and technical expertise is more important than product innovation.

» *Drawbacks*: The main weaknesses are inflexibility and slowness of reaction – Role Cultures find it hard to adjust to change.

Working in a Role Culture is frustrating for anybody wanting discretion and opportunity for innovation in their work.

» *Where you'll find it*: Local government and the civil service, and large insurance companies are prime examples. That said, their numbers are dwindling due to pressures for enhancing market competitiveness.

3. Task Culture

» *Overview*: Typically a Task Culture exists in a network-based orga-nization where co-operation between units is a necessary part of delivering a project. In Task Cultures, there is an emphasis on results and getting things done. Individuals are empowered with discretion and control over their work. These organizations are far more flexible and adaptable than Role Cultures.

» *How it works*: In a Task Culture, management is basically concerned with the continuous and successful solution to problems. The emphasis is on results and getting things done. Resources are given to the right people at whatever level who are brought together and given decision-making power to get on with the task. Power and respect come from individual knowledge rather than rank or position. The aspirations of the individual are integrated with the objectives of the organization.

» *Advantages*: The chief merits of a Task Culture are flexibility and adaptability.

Customers will normally see Task Cultures as highly responsive, if a little chaotic at times.

» *Drawbacks*: The price that Task Cultures pay for their flexibility is that economies of scale are seldom realized. That said, this is becoming less of an issue as computer communications and information systems facilitate sharing of information and co-ordination.

There can be an unhealthy level of competition between project leaders for available resources.

» *Where you'll find it*: Management consultancies, the product groups of marketing departments, and advertising agencies are prime examples.

4. Person Culture

» *Overview*: In this culture, the individual is the central point – there is no super-ordinate objective. Such structure as exists is only there to serve the individuals within it. The individuals are likely to have very strong values about how they should work.

» *How it works*: Power is only exercised by consent: expertise is more highly valued. People working in a Person Culture tend to have strong values about how they will work. They tend to see the organization as a base on which they can build their careers or pursue their own interests. They tend to leave the organization when it suits them, rather than at the organization's instigation.

» *Advantages*: A Person Culture may well be the only acceptable organization to particular groups – such as workers' co-operatives or where individuals basically work on their own but find some back-up useful.

» *Drawbacks*: Individuals with this orientation are very difficult to manage. Being specialists, they are often necessary to the organization but they have little allegiance to the company.

» *Where you'll find it*: A Person Culture is to be found wherever educated and articulate specialists come together because of common interest – solicitors, academic research, consultants etc. According to Charles Handy, attempting to control this type of organization is "like trying to herd a group of tom cats."

FACTORS THAT INFLUENCE THE CULTURE OF AN ORGANIZATION

Given the four cultural models – Power, Role, Task, and Person – what leads organizations to assume one form rather than any other? Charles Handy has identified six factors which would influence a choice of culture or structure for an organization. These are:

1 history and ownership
2 size
3 technology
4 goals and objectives
5 the environment
6 people.

1. History and ownership

The age of a company, its ownership, and its history will affect its culture, for example:

» family firms tend to become Power Cultures
» new organizations typically need to be either aggressive and independent (i.e. Power Culture) or flexible and adaptable (i.e. Task Culture), or possibly a combination of the two.

2. Size

According to Handy, size may be the single most important factor affecting the choice of structure or culture. For example, large organizations tend to be more formalized, and tend to develop specialist groups that will need systematic co-ordination. As a result, they are more likely to be role cultures.

3. Technology

The impact of technology on culture is not always obvious. Expensive, fast-changing technologies will leave the culture ambivalent between role and task. In general though, high investment in technologies will push cultures towards a role orientation. Low cost technology, e.g. readily available and powerful personal computers, may well support a Task Culture.

4. Goals and objectives

Different cultures tend to suit the pursuit of different goals and objectives. For example, a Role Culture can achieve growth, and a Power Culture can have strategic necessity as a goal. Role Cultures are unlikely to have extremely ambitious goals, whereas a Task Culture might well.

5. The environment

Handy uses the term "environment" to embrace the economic environment, the marketplace, the competitive scene and the wider geographical and societal environment. Here are some observations on these factors.

» Different nationalities prefer different organizational cultures.
» Some cultures are better suited to fast-changing environments than others. For example, the Task Culture is typically well suited to coping with changes in the market or the product.
» Diversity in the environment tends to favor Task Cultures.
» Standardization tends to favor Role Cultures.
» Threat or danger in the market – a merger battle for instance – is best handled by the Power Culture.

6. People

Different cultures call for different psychological contracts and so it is no surprise that certain types of people are likely to be happy and effective in one culture, and miserable, stressed, and ineffective in another. Handy suggests the following "matches":

» individuals with a low tolerance for ambiguity will prefer the tighter role prescriptions of the Role Culture;
» a high need for security will be best met in a Role Culture;
» a desire to establish a personal identity at work will be appropriate in a Power or Task Culture. However, in a Role Culture this would be seen as a "person" orientation and thought disruptive;
» the impact of individual skills and talents will be more marked in Power and Task Cultures than in a Role Culture; and
» individuals with low intelligence or low interpersonal skills are likely to fare best in a Role Culture.

CULTURE MATCHING WILL BECOME AS IMPORTANT AS JOB MATCHING

For companies of all sizes, finding the right candidates is becoming more expensive and more difficult. Although it is tempting to settle for a "near fit," many HR professionals are warning that finding someone who is the correct match for the firm's culture and values is at least as important as finding someone with the correct skill set.

CLUES TO UNCOVERING YOUR ORGANIZATION'S CULTURE

Imagine you were asked to describe your organization to an outsider. How would you answer the following questions?

» What five words would you use to describe your company?
» How does your company treat the people who work there?
» Who gets promoted?
» What behaviors get rewarded?
» What types of behavior get punished?
» Who fits in and who doesn't?
» Does your management encourage or discourage innovation and risk taking?
» Is rapid change the norm in your organization or is change generally resisted?
» Does the organization have a strong customer focus?

» How are decisions made? With a level of employee participation or is it down to senior management?

The answers you give will provide an insight into the real culture of your organization and some of its underlying values and norms.

CULTURE AS MEME MANAGEMENT

There is a growing body of opinion that cultural evolution can be modeled through the same basic principles of variation and selection that underlie biological evolution. This implies a shift from genes as units of biological information to a new type of unit of cultural information: *memes*. First coined by Richard Dawkins when updating Darwin's theory of natural selection in his groundbreaking book *The Selfish Gene*,[4] a meme is an idea, behavior, or skill that can be transferred from one person to another by imitation.

Memes are replicators and are all around us in our everyday lives, competing to get into our brains and minds. Examples include the way in which we copy ideas, inventions, songs, catch-phrases and stories from one another.

Dawkins listed the following three characteristics for any successful replicator.

» *Copying-fidelity*: the more faithful the copy, the more will remain of the initial pattern after several rounds of copying. If a painting is reproduced by making photocopies from photocopies, the underlying pattern will quickly become unrecognizable.
» *Fecundity*: the faster the rate of copying, the more the replicator will spread. An industrial printing press can churn out many more copies of a text than an office copying machine.
» *Longevity*: the longer any instance of the replicating pattern survives, the more copies can be made of it. A drawing made by etching lines in the sand is likely to be erased before anybody could have photographed or otherwise reproduced it.

Once humans learned to receive, copy, and retransmit memes, the rest, so the theory goes, is a foregone conclusion. We are the product of our memes just as we are the products of our genes, with memes, like genes, caring only for their own propagation.

The new science of memetics explains why we talk and think so much, why religions, cults, and ideologies have such power over us, and how our telephones, televisions, and computers could have been designed for the replication of memes.

Memetic competition shapes our minds and culture, just as natural selection has designed our bodies. But why should this matter to us and the organizations we work for? Well, for a start, it explains why the sexual adventures of an errant senior manager would grip the corporate imagination more than the latest set of financial figures.

CULTURE AS PERSONALITY

Forget all the talk about corporate culture. It's time to analyze your company's personality. According to marketing consultant Sandy Fekete,[5] companies can best be understood when thought of as people – as unique creatures with their own values, their own personalities, and sometimes, if her clients really get into the spirit, their own names.

"Most people assume that a company's personality matches its CEO's personality," says Fekete, "but that's not true. An organization has its own ways of being."

It may sound like psychobabble, but the idea behind the tool is fairly simple: an organization, like a person, has preferred ways of focusing energy, gathering information, making decisions, and structuring work. Once people inside an organization understand those preferences, they can do a better job of articulating their company's identity and values, and they can figure out better ways to work and to communicate. Some of her clients even elect "keepers of the personality" – volunteers who make sure that their organization is clear about the attributes that it prizes.

"Change comes from awareness," Fekete says. "Once you figure out who you are, you can begin to differentiate yourself from your competitors."

CULTURE IN RECESSIONARY TIMES

These days, it seems, impermanence is in and "jobs for life" are out. As the writer Naomi Klein puts it, "Offering employment – the steady kind, with benefits, holiday pay, a measure of security and maybe even union representation – has fallen out of economic fashion."[6]

It's difficult to imagine a scenario in which "jobs for life" could make anything like a meaningful comeback. Companies lose money – and they purge staff. Companies announce record profits – and they purge staff. The correlation between company profit and job growth, according to Klein, has never been weaker.

When we talk from a cultural perspective about companies downsizing, we need to recognize that downsizing can be seen both as a *response* to and as a *catalyst* of organizational culture change.

Certainly, the key drivers of organizational culture will tend to shape an organization's approach to downsizing. Why does the company exist? For whose benefit – shareholders, customers, the people that work there? What is the relationship between the organization and the people who work there? And so on.

It is a *catalyst* to the extent that the act of downsizing will often change the way people view the company. When a long-established, conservative, paternalistic life assurance company made over 100 of its workforce redundant a few years back – the first such redundancies in nearly 200 years of the company's existence – the impact on the company culture was immediate and almost tangible. "I trusted this company," said one senior manager that I spoke with at the time, "but I don't any more."

Downsizing can be a *response* to cultural factors in that it is a price to be paid for a set of decisions made by the company – and those decisions were of course made within a whole set of cultural perspectives.

It is, however, difficult to be specific about the exact nature of the link between downsizing and organizational culture. For one thing, there are many different approaches to downsizing taken by companies.

» There is, for example, a world of difference between *proactive* downsizing, which is planned in advance and usually integrated with a larger set of objectives, and *reactive* downsizing, which would be typified by last resort cost-cutting in the face of a looming crisis e.g. the massive reduction in headcount by the airline business following the series of terrorist attacks in September 2001.

» Reductions in headcount can be achieved forcibly through involuntary reductions, or cooperatively through voluntary redundancy, resignation incentives, job sharing etc.
» There are various methods used for deciding who stays and who goes. These range from the arbitrary to apparently objective criterion-based methods.
» Some companies are very open with their workers, others highly secretive.
» Some companies make staff redundant and immediately escort them off the premises, others allow workers more generous periods of notice.
» Some will fund outplacement support, others not.
» Some will use downsizing as a deliberately destabilizing event.

Each of these distinct ways of managing the downsizing process reflect as well as potentially reinforce or redefine the organizational culture.

TWENTY-FIRST CENTURY CULTURE SHAPERS

Fast Company magazine has identified five categories of people that it believes will shape and redefine organizational culture in the changing landscape of business.[7]

1 *Leaders*: Senior executives who create value through the power of their ideas, the depth of their commitment, and the authenticity of their character.
2 *Change agents*: Activists at every level who are determined to challenge the status quo and to make a positive difference for the future.
3 *Trendsetters*: Marketers and designers whose sense of style and powers of persuasion change what our world looks like.
4 *Disrupters*: Scientists and engineers whose breakthrough advances transform our sense of what's possible and rewrite the rules of competition and performance in business.
5 *Social entrepreneurs*: Dedicated innovators who are determined to tackle some of society's deepest challenges by embracing new ideas from business.

CULTURE AS EMERGENCE

We tend to regard organizational culture as reasonably stable. And yet, as we have discovered, culture is not a static entity but rather something which members of the organization, and particularly those in leadership roles, are continually creating, affirming, and expressing – sometimes explicitly, but usually tacitly. Organizational culture is partly the result of all the daily conversations and negotiations between the members of an organization. But it also develops in response to the wider business and social environment.

CULTURE AS A DRIVER OF POLICY FORMULATION

In companies with a strong value-based culture, it is possible to apply that culture to the formulation of specific policies. While this may seem like a common sense approach, relatively few companies explicitly ask how systems and procedures that are being considered square with the organization's culture. For example, all too many companies will drone on about their commitment to building a team-based culture, only to fatally undermine this commitment by continuing to have reward and promotion systems that are based explicitly on individual contribution. Asking whether a new practice actively supports the company's current or desired culture as a matter of course ensures that the organization's aims and practices are in alignment. The catch is that it does require a level of self-awareness that may be beyond many organizations.

METAPHOR AS A LENS FOR UNDERSTANDING CULTURE

Gareth Morgan, best-selling author and distinguished research professor at York University in Toronto, argues that the use of metaphor – for example, likening an organization to a machine – can be helpful in revealing aspects of organizational culture. "Images and metaphors are not only interpretive constructs or ways of seeing," he writes in his book *Images of Organization*,[8] "they also provide frameworks for action. They create insights that often allow us to act in ways that we may not have thought possible before." He then goes on to explore a rich range of metaphors (organizations as organisms, as brains, as cultures, as psychic prisons, as political systems etc.).

Let's examine one of these metaphors in a bit of detail. The machine metaphor, emphasizing as it does efficiency, consistency, reliability, a defined set of relationships between the various parts, and so on, has probably been the most widely used metaphor for many years. As a metaphor, it fitted well with the scientific management school created by Frederick Taylor in the early part of the twentieth century, and the mass production techniques that it spawned. Within this metaphor, human beings become cogs in the machine performing repetitive tasks. Should the cog fail, then it could be readily replaced by another with minimum disruption to the production process. The machine metaphor also brings with it a sense of worker alienation and a complete absence of flexibility.

CREATE YOUR OWN METAPHOR

Try it for yourself: if your organization was a vehicle of some description, what sort of vehicle might it be? A sleek Porsche? An old banger with bits falling off? An enormous oil tanker proceeding at a stately pace? Try drawing a picture of the vehicle.

However, Morgan is at pains to point out that metaphors are simply a way of discussing experience; they are not the experiences themselves. As such, their value is bound to be limited. Metaphors offer a distinctive means of filtering information about organizations. Viewing organizations as machines or as biological systems can provide some new insight about the nature of those organizations. However, although a new metaphor – organizations as chaotic systems for instance – may initially present a new and fresh view, the nature of the insight is inevitably partial and incomplete. A new metaphor can rapidly become as limiting a mindset as the more established, traditional metaphors.

KEY LEARNING POINTS

Roger Harrison identified four classifications of organizational culture: Power; Role; Task; and Person.

According to Charles Handy, there are six factors which influence how a culture develops: history and ownership; size; technology; goals and objectives; the environment; and people.

NOTES

1 http://www.alliesconsulting.com/resources/articles/idinflcult.html
2 Handy, C. (1989) *The Age of Unreason*. Hutchinson, London.
3 Handy, C. (1993) *Understanding Organizations*, 4th edn. Penguin.
4 Dawkins, R. (1976) *The Selfish Gene*. Oxford University Press, Oxford.
5 Muoio, A. (2000) "Companies are people too." *Fast Company* **36**, July.
6 Klein, N. (2000) *No Logo*. Flamingo, London.
7 *Fast Company* (2001), **52**, November.
8 Morgan, G. (1986) *Images of Organization*. Sage, Newbury Park, California.

NOTES

Lessons from Best Practice

There is no such thing as a best practice culture. Different companies of necessity will have different cultures; the crunch question is whether a company's culture enables or stands in the way of an organization achieving its objectives. This chapter describes how a number of companies successfully addressed cultural issues.

- » Case studies:
  - » EDS
  - » Nissan
  - » Scandinavian Airlines
  - » St Luke's
- » Common themes in effective culture change
- » Key learning points

"An individual without information cannot take responsibility; an individual who is given information cannot help but take responsibility."

Jan Carlzon, former president of Scandinavian Airlines

"This ability to perceive the limitations of one's own culture and to develop the culture adaptively is the essence and ultimate challenge of leadership."

Edgar Schein, in his book Organizational Culture and Leadership

An organization's culture is expressed and transmitted in numerous ways, including:

» the formal statements of philosophy, values, charter, and credo;
» the behavior modeled by management;
» the criteria used for reward, status, selection, promotion, and termination;
» the stories, legends, myths, and parables about key people and events;
» what leaders pay attention to, measure, and control;
» leader reactions to critical incidents and crises that threaten survival, challenge norms, and test values;
» how the organization is designed and structured; and
» organizational systems and procedures.

It is how organizations manage these elements during periods of transition that often seems to determine whether they achieve their goals. In this section, we will look at three organizations and how they have tackled – with varying levels of success – challenges facing their businesses. Each case study will be followed by a brief description of key lessons or insights to be drawn.

EDS

The company
Launched by one-time US presidential candidate Ross Perot in Dallas, Texas back in 1962, EDS (Electronic Data Systems Corporation) is a leading global services company. In setting up the company, Perot

backed his belief that other organizations would hire a company to handle all of their computer operations. This was a radical notion at the time, being well before the concept of outsourcing entered the business consciousness.

EDS went on to become a dominant player, growing rapidly after carmaker General Motors acquired it in 1984. Under GM's wing, EDS established operations in 42 countries and grew to become a $14bn giant before it split off in 1996.

But following the split off from GM in 1996, EDS was too slow for the IT marketplace, amongst other things missing out on the onset of the Internet phenomenon. Over the next three years, a number of faster, nimbler start-ups ate away at EDS's market share. Also, IBM launched its own IT services division and rapidly became the market leader. So by 1999, when new CEO Dick Brown joined the company, EDS was floundering.

Brown was the first outsider to lead EDS in the company's history. He arrived with an unambiguous message: "A company's culture is really the behavior of its people. And leaders get the behavior they tolerate."

The story

The symbolism was stark and easy to interpret. When Dick Brown arrived at EDS from being CEO at Britain's Cable & Wireless, he found that the previous CEO had had his phone lines cut to avoid incoming calls.

There were many other indications of corporate out-of-touchness. It took Brown six telephone calls to find out how many people were employed by the company. Nobody could provide him with the previous month's sales figures. When he wanted to send an e-mail to everybody in the company, he was told that it was not possible with the company's technology.

One hundred days after he joined, Brown took six of his top executives to the New York Stock Exchange. While they were there, Brown vowed to restore the fortunes of the company. He went on to commit the company to achieving some very challenging financial and business targets. But he also realized that those targets meant little in themselves unless he set about addressing a much "softer" issue – EDS's culture.

In a recently published article,[1] he described his thinking: "Most business leaders are afraid to talk about culture. They're far more comfortable with numbers. While I am very numbers focused, you can't change a business with numbers. Numbers are the end result. You change a business by changing the behavior of its people."

The same article goes on to describe how Brown quickly signaled that he would not put up with the old culture of information hoarding and rampant individualism:

> "In one of his first meetings, Brown asked 30 top managers to e-mail him the three most important things that they could do to improve the company and the three most important things that he could do. He made his request on a Monday and asked the managers to e-mail him their action items by the end of the week – at the latest. 'I was interested in what they'd send, but I was more interested in when they'd send it,' Brown says. 'This was a litmus test on urgency.' Ninety percent of the managers waited until Friday afternoon to reply to Brown. 'It never crossed their minds that they could email me within the hour,' Brown says. 'They just did it at the last minute. And that's the message that they sent to their people: Do it at the last minute. In the end, almost all of them loaded up on what I needed to do. They were pretty light on what they needed to do.' "

Today, most of those managers are gone from EDS.

Brown also put in place a set of practices – internally dubbed "operating mechanisms" – that were intended to create a company-wide culture based on instant feedback and direct, unfiltered communication.

Another problem Brown and his leadership team had to face was the company's organizational structure. Over the years, EDS had subdivided into 48 separate units, each with its own management team and its own financial accountability. Unfortunately, the individual operating units refused to communicate or co-operate with each other, and as a result EDS had no single overarching strategy. By no stretch of the imagination could the company be called market-facing or coherent – instead the operating units were rolling out overlapping and sometimes duplicated offerings.

Brown's response was to set up *Project Breakaway*, drawing on a team of seven leaders from different parts of EDS, each with a different industry expertise. Their task: to draft a blueprint for a client-centered organizational structure. Brown's secondary goal: to help EDS break away from the old ways of doing business. After six weeks, the project team presented a new model in which the 48 units were cut to just four lines of business, all of them focused directly on the client.

Brown's recipe seems to have worked. Over the past couple of years, EDS has set up very profitable partnerships with many of the technology sector's key players – Cisco, Dell, EMC, Microsoft, and so on. In October 2000, EDS beat off competition from IBM to win a $6.9bn contract from the US Navy. And in July 2001, the company announced a 17% increase in its quarterly profits, a 7.5% rise in revenue, and an $80bn backlog of signed contracts.

Analysis

In retrospect, EDS's period of GM-sponsored success turned out to be more of a curse than a blessing. The financial underpinning that came from GM fostered a culture of complacency and unwillingness to change. There was no overriding incentive for individual operating units to co-operate, and senior managers had grown aloof.

As in so many cases, the EDS turnaround needed a new leader with a fresh vision. In a *Fast Company* magazine article,[2] Dick Brown gave the following insights into how he had changed a lagging company into a high performer.

» *The Straight Stuff, Straight From the Top:* Every other week, Brown sends an e-mail message to all 128,000 EDS staff members, telling them where EDS is going, how it will get there, and what challenges lie ahead. Each e-mail is also an explicit invitation to get into dialogue, since anybody at EDS can write back to him.

» *Go off-site to get close-up*: Two or three times a year, Brown convenes the company's senior executives for a three-day meeting. Leaders learn how to team by teaming.

» *Nowhere to run to, nowhere to hide*: Once a month, the top 125 worldwide leaders participate in an hour-long conference call, in which the CFO goes through the previous month's numbers for each executive. The call serves to make every company member's performance transparent.

» *Money doesn't talk, it screams*: Brown has introduced a pay-for-performance system that ranks every employee. Top performers are rewarded; poor performers are given the opportunity to get better.

» *Color-coded clients: go, caution, crisis*: The company's "Service Excellence Dashboard" is a Web-enabled tool that lets clients rate EDS. It forces speed and collaboration.

» *Here's your coachable moment!*: Brown is a big believer in delivering real-time feedback, which he calls "coachable moments." The phrase has entered EDS's lexicon: "May I give you a coachable moment?" The goal is to make coaching a part of everyday behavior.

NISSAN

The organization

Established in 1933 to manufacture and sell small Datsun passenger cars and auto parts, nowadays Nissan is engaged in corporate activities on a global scale. The company operates 20 manufacturing companies in 16 countries around the world with a combined annual production volume of approximately 2.6 million units.

In March 1999, Nissan and Renault signed a comprehensive alliance agreement aimed at strengthening Nissan's financial position and at the same time achieving profitable growth for both companies.

The story

In 1999, Japanese car giant Nissan was in a bad way. So bad that when Renault, the French car company, took a 36.8% stake in Nissan, business commentators were calling the task facing Carlos Ghosn, Renault's appointment into the role of Chief Operating Officer, "mission impossible."

Yet two years later, losses of ¥684bn ($6.1bn) had been turned into a profit of ¥331bn. Ghosn described the transformation as the company moving from the emergency ward to the recovery room.

The Nissan story is not just an example of an impressive corporate recovery, but also a case study of how to work in an alliance, and of how a foreigner can shake up a failing Japanese company, despite a perceived cultural gulf. That said, Ghosn consistently plays down the cultural aspect: "I don't know what is a Japanese company," he has said. "As with anywhere else, 'you just get bad ones and great ones.'"

The real challenge now has been to change attitudes at Nissan, from top to bottom and from design right through to sales. One of the first things that Ghosn noticed on assuming his new role was that nobody seemed to take responsibility when things went wrong. Managers blamed the strength of the yen or the poor state of Japan's economy for the company's plight, ignoring the fact that competitors such as Honda and Toyota were prospering.

An early initiative by the new COO was to form cross-functional teams to work on ways to break down barriers between departments. But when he outlined his recovery plan to his senior managers, there were distinct pockets of resistance; however, he began to see changes as a number of key executives agreed that the plan had merit. These days, he gives a very positive assessment of Japanese managers: "When you get a clear strategy and communicate your priorities, it's a pleasure working in Japan. The Japanese are so organized and know how to make the best of things. They respect leadership."

Analysis

Ghosn has described the challenge of managing an alliance between two very different cultures as dealing with "the contradiction between synergy and identity." Too much synergy and you lose identity. "Identity matters," he says, "because it is the basis of motivation, and motivation is the fuel that companies run on." In his view, it remains vital that Renault people identify with their company and brand, just as Nissan staff should still do with theirs.

There is a view of alliances, particularly in the car industry, that they too often achieve the opposite of synergy. Two plus two can equal three. It is to Ghosn's credit that he has avoided that sub-optimal trap.

At a broader level, the 1990s were tricky times for many Japanese businesses. Company leaders came to realize that the bursting of the bubble economy and the overhanging recession of 1993 were more than temporary setbacks – they were signs of substantial problems with Japan's long-term competitiveness.

The heart of the crisis was steadily diminishing levels of white-collar productivity, a problem worldwide but a particularly severe one for Japanese businesses. This is a problem that Japan continues to grapple with today. In these ultra-competitive times, not even the most efficient companies can sustain the high overheads they have accumulated. As a result, many companies are beginning to downsize or look for ways to trim the size of their payrolls. But restructuring will not be enough. Japanese leaders must find a solution that combines short-term cuts with long-term innovations in generating productivity, job flexibility, and continued worker commitment.

SCANDINAVIAN AIRLINES

The company

In 1981, Jan Carlzon became president of Scandinavian Airlines (SAS) at a time when many other airlines were losing what were at the time record amounts of money. He replaced SAS's production orientation with customer focus, emphasizing to all employees that they were in a service business. "We used to fly airplanes; now we must learn how to fly people," he explained. In less than a year, under his leadership, SAS returned to high profitability and became a world-class airline. SAS won numerous international awards based on its service innovations in the 1980s and became one of the most profitable airlines in the world.

Carlzon left SAS in November 1993 to become chairman, CEO and part-owner of Transpool AB, an integrated leisure, travel, and airline company.

The story

"Thirty thousand passengers, a lot of them on business, fly SAS every day and come face to face with our people about five times a trip, and that's a hundred fifty thousand encounters a day, moments of truth that can make or break us and I don't control a single one of them."

Jan Carlzon

In 1986, Jan Carlzon wrote a book, *Moments of Truth*.[3] And what is a moment of truth? According to Carlzon, "Anytime a customer comes into contact with any aspect of a business, however remote, is an opportunity to form an impression.''

From this simple concept, Jan Carlzon took an airline that was failing and turned it into one of the most respected airlines in his industry.

Some examples of moments of truth in the airline business are:

» when a customer calls to make a reservation to take a flight;
» when a customer checks in;
» when a customer is greeted at the gate;
» when a customer is taken care of by the flight attendants on board the aircraft;
» when a customer is greeted at their destination; and
» crucially, when a customer presents a problem that needs addressing.

Of course, moments of truth are not unique to the airline industry – every industry, every business, every worker has their set of ''moments.'' Most of them revolve around interaction between people – customers and employees.

At SAS, Carlzon was determined to create an organizational culture that would encourage and enable his people to manage their moments of truth better than any of their competitors.

To achieve this goal, he made a number of sweeping changes. These included:

» choosing and communicating goals that everybody in the business could understand and rally around;
» reducing the numbers of middle management numbers dramatically and making the remainder responsible for breaking down the inter-departmental barriers which he saw them guilty of creating in the first place;
» reversing the normal pyramid view of organizations that shows the boss at the top and the people who actually meet customers at the bottom. In Carlzon's view, the only justification for management is that it should enable and facilitate the people in customer contact to do their jobs well. So he drew the chart with himself at the bottom, the customer at the top, and the customer contact people just below them – a reverse pyramid;

» revamping pay and conditions for his workers so that they explicitly helped to foster the new behavior set; and

» explicitly turning control over to the ticket agents, cabin attendants, and others who really need it. "If a passenger has a problem," he said, "don't worry about protocol or a few pennies. Just fix it. And I will back you 100%."

Analysis

Jan Carlzon is an example of a leader who helped a company achieve a brilliant turnaround success in double-quick time.

How did he do it? Leaders like Carlzon are always to be seen around the company. They're always talking with and listening to customers. They are forever encouraging their people to be creative about helping customers to solve problems. Crucially, they don't get seduced into trying to provide all of the answers.

Much of Carlzon's thinking was revolutionary in the 1980s. Although his views about how a company can achieve extraordinary levels of customers by flattening the pyramid, empowering front-line workers, communicating business information openly, using reward systems to positively encourage various employee behaviors etc. have been absorbed into mainstream thinking (and to a lesser degree into main-stream practice), Carlzon's electrifying impact on SAS shows just how much a visionary leader can achieve in a very short period of time.

JAN CARLZON: FRONT-LINE CUSTOMER SERVICE IS STILL IMPORTANT[4]

Speaking at a quality conference, Jan Carlzon shared a personal example of the importance of front-line customer service:

"I went to stay at a hotel in London for the sixteenth time. When I arrived, the clerk asked for my name, then confirmed my reservation, then asked me to fill out a lengthy form. Perfect service, but it had nothing to do with individual customer service.

"Could you imagine if the manager had called his employees together in the morning and said 'Today Jan Carlzon is coming.

He's been here 15 times. I also remember he likes antique fairs.' So, when I arrive, the clerk asks for my name. I tell him and he says 'Welcome, Mr. Carlzon. We are proud to have you here for the sixteenth time. Please sign this form that we already completed for you from past records. By the way, we put some brochures about antique fairs in your room because we know that you are interested in them.'

"The difference is obvious. Business is not about selling the second or third time. You have to concentrate on *user satisfaction*.

"In the 1980s we used to: 'See a *Customer* in each *Individual*.'

"These days, we must: 'See an *Individual* in each *Customer*.' "

ST LUKE'S

The organization

Although formally launched on St Luke's day in October 1995 – St Luke being the patron saint of creativity and healing – the company's roots can be traced back to the early 1990s when Andy Law and David Abraham, two senior staff from the London office of the US advertising agency Chiat Day, joined a team of people drawn from Chiat Day's international network that was given the task of renewing the company's sense of purpose. At the time, their proposal that Chiat Day should become an explicitly ethical advertising company was thrown out by Chiat Day's founder, Jay Chiat. Nonetheless, Law and Abraham took the opportunity to revamp the operating practices of the London office by introducing new ways of working.

All went well until 1995, when one evening Jay Chiat called Law to tell him that the whole company, including the London office, had just been sold. Law was asked to merge the London office with the operations of a rival agency. Law and Abraham, with the backing of the creative team from the London office operation, decided they would rather go it alone. Following negotiations with the new owners, Law and Abraham bought the London operation for £1 plus a share of the profits, worth £1.2 million, over seven years.

The story

When they bought the company, Law and Abraham could have kept the equity and become millionaires – on paper at least. Instead, they decided to take the opportunity to create a new kind of company, one in which:

» the company's ownership reflected everyone's contribution to the business;
» the company was built on a set of relationships rather than a hierarchy; and
» open management would be used, not traditional command and control.

To achieve this model, approximately 30% of the company's shares were distributed to employees in equal portions, regardless of salary, rank, or length of service. The remainder of the shares were held in a trust with the aim that the trust will always have a majority.

In fact, employees play an enormous part in the company's development. This is clearly seen in the fact that St Luke's is governed by a five person board known as the Quest. One board member is the company's lawyer, two are senior employees, with the remaining two elected by a vote of the workforce. The Quest is the company's primary decision-making vehicle on employment-related issues – maternity leave, sick leave, employment contracts, and so on. It meets at fortnightly intervals, and any staff member can come along as an observer.

ANDY LAW ON CULTURE[5]

"Do you work somewhere that has a strong company culture?

"What do I mean by that? 'Company culture?' Actually, it's quite a vague concept, weightless yet omnipresent, ardently defended yet invisible.

"You will know if you have a company culture. You will know because it will be referred to by your co-workers ('Don't worry, it always takes a few weeks to get into place.'). You will know because you will feel acceptance or rejection ('She's just not one of us. She's too ... um ... er ... you know.').

You will know because your boss will tell you ('It's OK, what you're doing. Don't get me wrong. It's just that it's not the way we do things around here.').

"All workplaces have codes of conduct, histories, habits, routines, nicknames, catch-phrases, myths, mission statements, Chairman's statements, objectives, strategies, systems, procedures. Merge them all together and you can get what might be passed off as company culture. But the real thing is decidedly different and is distinctive from the many false cultures that can be found operating deep within companies . . .

"I guess at this point I should assert my own definitions. I think a culture is very different from a vision, and both of these are very different from a mission. They ought to be defined, because then their role is made clear. By that, I am not suggesting that all companies need a vision, or a mission, or indeed a culture in order to be successful. I would, however, say that with them, you are likely to be more successful.

"A vision is something you aim for. A long shot that you know you will never fully achieve. Or if you do, it would dramatically change the company you are in. It is an endless pursuit. Our vision at St Luke's is 'To Open Minds.'

"A mission is the method by which you aim to reach your vision. Ours is 'By Creating Fascination.'"

St Luke's style is also reflected in the working environment. Unlike most companies where the biggest offices go to the most senior staff, St Luke's structures its office around its clients, each of whom have a themed and specially decorated "brand meeting room" dedicated to them. Most of the rest of the building is made up of shared spaces with staff working at large common tables on a "hot desking" principle. Nobody is allowed to bag a permanent spot. All resources – like computers and mobile phones – are shared.

Analysis

The model that Abraham and Law put in place was brilliantly suited to the company's purpose. St Luke's is an ethical company that produces advertising which is about more than selling products. Clients are encouraged to take a broader view of their social role as a way of unlocking hidden brand value. It is also recognized as one of the most creative agencies in the business, something which is due in no small measure to the working environment and employee attitude that the company has engendered.

There are issues, however. An open management style requires a lot of patience. Command and control might not be pretty but it is quick – at St Luke's everything has to be negotiated.

Continuing growth also presents its own dilemmas. Any company that grows very fast can find it a challenge to get new employees to buy into the prevailing culture.

On the other hand, whether the model developed at St Luke's has the resilience to cope with a downturn in its business fortunes (the company has enjoyed continuous growth since its creation) remains to be seen. In the meantime, St Luke's makes a compelling case study for any business leader seeking a new approach.

BEST PRACTICE: PULLING IT ALL TOGETHER

"Organizational culture is the key to organizational excellence . . . and the function of leadership is the creation and management of culture."

Edgar Schein, Organizational Culture and Leadership

So what can we conclude from the case studies in this section? Here are five key themes that run through most, if not all, of the examples we have looked at:

1. The organization cannot learn anything new if the leaders themselves do not.

One of the critical factors in understanding a corporate culture is the degree to which it is leader-centric. If you are the leader yourself, the culture of your company is likely to reflect your personality, both your positive qualities and your faults. If you tend to avoid conflict or sweep it under the carpet, you can expect to see similar approaches played out by your people. The behavior that is modeled by the leader and the management team profoundly shapes the culture and practices of the organization. The tone of the corporate culture is set by the behavior of members of the senior team, their reactions in a crisis, what they routinely talk about or focus on etc.

Any leader of an organization may have at some point to face the possibility that their organization's culture is not what they would wish. But remember that it is the leader's own cultural assumptions that both enable and constrain what organizations are able to do and achieve. It is only when a leader recognizes that they themselves might be the problem that they are given a chance to become part of the solution.

CULTURAL CHECKLIST FOR LEADERS

Throughout this book, we have consistently returned to a key theme – the critical role that organizational leaders play in determining the type of culture that prevails in their company.

Leaders need to be constantly alert to their company's culture. Interpreting and understanding organizational culture is important for business leaders because it affects strategic development, productivity, and learning at all levels. This is relatively easy when a leader is new to an organization.

The bottom line for leaders is that if they do not become conscious of the cultures in which they are embedded, those cultures will manage them.

The following set of questions is designed to help a leader maintain an alert awareness of cultural issues. The list is not comprehensive, but it is a useful starting point that will help a leader identify the unique factors in an organizational culture.

» Are the strategic objectives and the culture in alignment?
» What are the key cultural leverage points for organizational change?

- » Are there any cultural misalignments that have emerged from mergers and acquisitions?
- » How do key members of the management team fit with the culture you need to create?
- » How can you attract and retain employees?
- » Can anyone ask a question, or is it just certain groups that can do this?
- » Are mistakes encouraged or forgiven if people learn from them?
- » Do people learn from mistakes?
- » How do new entrants to your company describe it? Where does their view differ from your own?
- » Do people act or feel in a positive way or do people act and feel in negative ways?
- » Is there any pride in the workplace?
- » Will people follow a leader willingly?
- » Is everyone encouraged to think and contribute to problem-solving in the organization, or are only certain groups assigned that responsibility?
- » Who is really in charge? Is authority centralized, or is there decision-making autonomy and decentralization?
- » Why do people stay in their jobs, rather than apply elsewhere?
- » What is the level of staff turnover? What are the reasons for this?
- » How is conflict handled?
- » Does the organization operate using a long-term vision, or is everything decided at the level of short-term vision?
- » Do people use collaboration and co-operation regularly for problem-solving and decision-making at all levels?

2. It is crisis not comfort that propels significant cultural change

When all is going well for a business, changing the formula is often the last thing on anybody's mind. There has to be at least a troubling sense that something is different, and that things aren't working the way they used to. Perhaps customers' attitudes toward you are different, or maybe competitors that you wrote off or hardly knew existed are stealing business from you.

An organizational crisis is often the spur to bringing in a new leader, somebody who can bring something different to the party. These new leaders, unhampered by past decisions, old loyalties, or corporate blind spots, are more likely to have the clarity of vision to realize that the corporate formula (and hence the corporate culture) needs to change radically.

3. Be patient: corporate culture doesn't change overnight

Although changes in behavior can be brought about quickly, other changes – in roles, relationships, values, norms, attitudes, communication patterns, and so on – require a lot longer. These things are deeply ingrained in people, and it generally takes considerable time and experience working in the new ways for people to become comfortable with them. Major, long-lasting changes take time, and organizations typically must pass through a period of uncertainty as they make the transition from where they were to where they want to go. This period of transition is often painful, but can be made easier if people have a clear vision to work towards, and if they are given help and on-going support.

4. There is no such thing as the ideal culture

There is no right or wrong culture, no better or worse culture, except in relation to what the organization is trying to do. A team of fire fighters will necessarily have a different set of operating patterns to an advertising agency.

5. Other common elements that help organizations change successfully

A study of companies that made large-scale, successful changes found the following common elements:

» establishment of clear objectives for the change;
» effective meshing of the different subcultures by encouraging the evolution of common goals, common language, and common procedures for solving problems;

» agreement of the majority of people in the organization that change is needed;
» involvement of people affected by change in planning and carrying it out;
» consistency: if a leader is unaware and inconsistent then confusion ensues;
» anticipation of problems created by change and steps taken to solve them (e.g. training in new skills provided, salary systems harmonized etc.);
» placing of much energy and effort into communicating aspects of the change – briefings, newsletters etc.;
» phased and carefully planned implementation of change; and
» effective control of recruitment and internal selection processes: who gets promoted and who doesn't sends a powerful message to the organization.

FINALLY, A WORD OF WARNING: IF IT AIN'T BROKE...

Case studies by their nature focus on organizations that needed to do something concrete to address and resolve problems that posed some level of threat to them. Against this backdrop, it can be tempting for a business leader to look to make cultural interventions in their companies even where there is no particular imperative to do so.

If the culture is already firmly established, and if an organization is performing effectively in its marketplace, then the most effective contribution that an MD can make might well be to act as a guardian and reinforcer of the current culture.

KEY LEARNING POINTS IN THIS CHAPTER
» Overview of section
» Case studies
  » EDS
  » Nissan
  » Scandinavian Airlines
» Common themes in effective culture change

NOTES

1 Breen, B. (2001) 'How EDS Got Its Groove Back.' *Fast Company*, October. The full article can be found at www.fastcompany.com/online/51/eds.html

2 ibid.

3 Carlzon, J. (1987) *Moments of Truth*. Harper & Row, New York.

4 Taken from the Website of Process Quality Associates Inc., http://www.pqa.net/page04.htm

5 Derived from: Law, A. (1999) *Open Minds*. Orion, London. In the US, the book was published under the title *Creative Company*.

Key Concepts and Thinkers

This section contains a selective glossary of key terms, key concepts and key thinkers associated with organizational culture.

"If you work in a company with more than four employees that's been in business for more than two months, you have an organizational or company culture."

Russ Giles[1]

Like many other business subjects, the theory and practice of organizational culture have a language all their own. Here is a selective glossary of some of the key terms, key concepts, and key thinkers associated with the subject.

Adhocracy – A non-bureaucratic networked organization with a highly organic organizational design.

Artifacts – Artifacts are everything we might see, hear, or feel within an organization. They include: the physical environment; all visible behaviors; the way people dress; rituals and ceremonies; published documents; the technology used; commonly used language and jargon; status symbols such as cars; job titles; and so on.

Business web – A term coined by Tapscott, Ticoll, and Lowy in their book *Digital Capital* to describe a series of new business forms and models that are being spawned by Internet-based partnerships or alliances. They define a business web, or "b-web" for short, as "a distinct system of suppliers, distributors, commerce services providers, infrastructure providers and customers that use the Internet for their primary business communications and transactions." Although alliance-based, a b-web typically has an identifiable lead partner which formally orchestrates their strategies and processes.

Communities of practice – Groups that form within an organization, typically of their own accord, where members are drawn to one other by a common set of needs that may be both professional and social. Compared to project teams, communities of practice are voluntary, longer-lived, have no specific deliverable, and are responsible only to themselves. Because they are free of formal strictures and hierarchy within an organization, they can be viewed as subversive.

Core competencies – The key strengths of an organization (sometimes called distinctive capabilities). Gary Hamel and C.K. Prahalad, authors of *Competing for the Future*,[2] define core competencies as "a bundle of skills and technologies (rather than a simple or discrete skill or technology) that enables the company to provide a particular benefit to customers.''

Corporate culture - This is the pattern of basic assumptions that a given group has invented, discovered, or developed in learning to cope with its problems of external adaptation and internal integration, and that have worked well enough to be considered valid, and therefore taught to new members as the correct way to perceive, think, and feel in relation to those problems.

Covert culture - Term coined by Gerard Egan, Professor of Organization Development and Psychology at Loyola University of Chicago, to describe those elements of organizational culture that are, in his words, ''not in the private consciousness of the members of the institution, not in the public consciousness of members of the institution, not written down, not named or noted in some public forum, only partially understood, not celebrated in some public way, not discussed in any public forum, not challenged or perhaps not even open to challenge, considered undiscussable in public forums and at times so undiscussable that even their undiscussability is undiscussable.''

Cultural diagnostics - Cultural diagnosis is a vital part of the strategic process because it allows us to become aware of the filters that we use to process our experience, both as individuals and as members of organizations, and the degree of ''selectivity'' that is involved in interpreting those experiences. It is a complex area, not least because it deals directly with the foibles that we have as human beings.

Cultural fit - Building and sustaining a corporate culture that fits your needs requires a critical mass of employees who are committed to the culture's core beliefs and values. It is much easier to hire people with those traits than to change their personalities, beliefs, and behaviors once they are hired. Ask questions in the interviews and listen carefully to their stories about previous work experiences. Listen for cultural fit: you may be hiring the technical or professional skills you need but damaging your chances of building a strong culture.

Cultural integration - Some companies have a strong dominant culture that is pervasive throughout the organization, across business units and regions. An organization of this type is said to possess a high level of cultural integration.

Cultural web – A useful concept in which the organization is understood in terms of the routines, rituals, stories, structures, and systems that exist within it. It can be used to elicit the organizational paradigm because each component of the cultural web provides clues about taken-for-granted organizational assumptions.

Culture carriers – People in an organization that is going through a period of change who see the new direction and feel comfortable moving in that direction.

Culture destabilizers – Factors which can have a negative impact on an organization's morale and sense of security during times of change e.g. layoffs, sudden termination, executives getting big bonuses while cutting others' positions.

Culture reinforcers – Factors which reinforce a sense that an organization is concerned for the well-being of its workers, even in times of difficulty. Examples include: voluntary reductions; open communication; shared pain (e.g. cuts across all levels); explicit criteria for "who stays, who goes."

Discontinuities – One-off changes in the marketplace that force radical organizational change.

Distinctive capabilities – See Core competencies.

Downsizing – Restructuring an organization in a declining market where the level of resources (manpower, support functions etc.) are inappropriate to meeting current customer needs.

e-lancers – Independent contractors connected through personal computers and electronic networks. These electronically connected freelancers join together into fluid and temporary networks to produce and sell goods and services.

Espoused values – This is what an organization says it believes. Sometimes this will be manifest in the artifacts of the organization e.g. an espoused value that open communication is important may show itself in the form of regular briefings for employees, or the way an office is laid out, or in the content of the corporate mission statement. Sometimes, however, these values will be espoused but not enacted. These moments of discrepancy between what an organization says it believes and what it does in practice are in themselves highly indicative of the type of organizational culture that prevails.

Fayol, Henry – Perhaps more than anybody, Henri Fayol (1841–1925), a mining engineer and manager by profession, defined the nature and working patterns of the twentieth-century organization. In his book, *General and Industrial Management*, published in 1916, Fayol laid down 14 principles of management (see Chapter 3 for more details). Fayol also characterized the activities of a commercial organization into six basic elements: technical; commercial; financial; security; accounting; and management. The management function, Fayol believed, consisted of planning, organizing, commanding, co-ordinating and controlling. Many practicing managers today would probably identify similar elements as the core of their activities.

Gap analysis – Method for exploring the gap between current reality and the vision of the organization, both in terms of external customer needs and internal capabilities.

Globalization – The integration of economic activity across national or regional boundaries, a process that has been accelerated by the impact of information technology.

Glocalization – The creation of products or services intended for the global market, but customized to suit the local culture.

Herzberg, Frederick – In his book *Motivation to Work*,[3] Herzberg coined the terms "hygiene factors" and "motivational factors" as a basis for exploring what motivated people to work well and happily.

Hofstede, Geert – Geert H. Hofstede was born in the Netherlands in 1928. He is currently Emeritus Professor of Organizational Anthropology and International Management at Maastricht University in the Netherlands. Hofstede is best known for his work on four dimensions of cultural variability, commonly referred to as Hofstede's Dimensions.

Internal capabilities or competencies – What the organization is good at. Something an organization can do that its potential competitors cannot.

Internal constraints – Factors that can inhibit an organization's ability to achieve desired outcomes. These factors include the level of resources available, knowledge of new markets and products, the cultural adaptability of the organization to new opportunities etc.

Jaques, Elliott – For over 50 years, Jaques has consistently advocated the need for a scientific approach to understanding work systems. He argues that there is a "widespread, almost universal, under-estimation of the impact of organization on how we go about our business." He believes, for example, that rapid change in people's behavior is achieved less through altering their psychological make-up and more by revising organizational structures and managerial leading practices. His book *Requisite Organization* challenges many current assumptions about effective organizations, particularly in the field of hierarchy of which Jaques is a fan. Some find his theories indigestible, but for those who persist there is a wealth of challenging material that undermines much conventional organizational wisdom.

Learning organization – Peter Senge characterizes learning organizations as places where "people continually expand their capacity to create the results they truly desire, where new and expansive patterns of thinking are nurtured, where collective aspiration is set free, and where people are continually learning how to learn together." He also acknowledges that the idea of a learning organization is a vision.

Maslow, Abraham – Abraham Maslow remains one of the most widely known experts on human behavior and motivation. His psychological perspectives on management, such as the hierarchy of needs, are still studied today in business schools all over the world. Maslow's most influential business book, *Eupsychian Management*,[4] is a stimulating but not always easy read that demonstrates clearly why Maslow was an unparalleled thinker and innovator in applying human behavior to the workplace.

Meme – First coined by Richard Dawkins when updating Darwin's theory of natural selection in his groundbreaking book *The Selfish Gene*,[5] a meme is an idea, behavior, or skill that can be transferred from one person to another by imitation. Memes are replicators and are all around us in our everyday lives, competing to get into our brains and minds. Examples include the way in which we copy ideas, inventions, songs, catch-phrases and stories from one another.

Mission – In theory, mission statements should capture the essence of the organization, those things about it which are truly unique and provide the platform from which the organization can create the future. Management writers sometimes refer to this as establishing purpose or strategic intent. The statement takes the form of a formal declaration of what an organization is all about, rooted in a clear understanding of reality. In practical terms, mission statements rarely live up to very much and are often little more than a collection of management buzzwords that are not rooted in organizational reality.

Moments of truth - Term coined by Jan Carlzon, former president of Scandinavian Airlines (SAS), to describe those critical occasions when a customer comes into contact with any aspect of a business, and there is an opportunity to create an impression, positive or negative. From this simple concept, Carlzon took an airline that was failing and turned it into one of the most respected airlines in his industry.

Morgan, Gareth - A Professor at York University in Toronto, Morgan is a best-selling author, speaker, and consultant on managing change. He argues that the use of metaphor, for example likening an organization to a machine, can be helpful in revealing aspects of organizational life. For the use of metaphor implies a way of thinking and a way of seeing that pervade how we understand our world generally. In his book *Images of Organization*,[6] he explores a rich range of metaphors (organizations as organisms, as brains, as cultures, as psychic prisons, as political systems etc.).

Organizational Behavior (OB) - The study of human behavior, attitudes, and performance within an organizational setting. OB draws on theory, methods, and principles from such disciplines as psychology, sociology, and cultural anthropology to learn about individual perception, values, learning capabilities, and actions while working with groups and within the total organization. OB also can involve analyzing the external environment's effect on the organization and its learning resources, missions, objectives, and strategies.

Organizational culture - Defined by Edgar Schein, a professor at MIT who is considered one of the "founders" of organizational psychology, as "a pattern of shared basic assumptions that the group learned as it solved its problems of external adaptation and internal integration, that has worked well enough to be considered valid and, therefore, to be taught to new members as the correct way to perceive, think, and feel in relation to those problems." Schein's definition brings together many of the ideas and concepts expressed in that earlier list of definitions, but putting particular emphasis on shared, taken-for-granted basic assumptions held by the member of the group or organization.

Organization Development (OD) – According to Richard Beckhard, writing in his book *Organization Development: strategies and models*,[7] "OD is an effort that is (1) planned, (2) organization-wide, and (3) managed from the top, to increase (4) organizational effectiveness and health, through (5) planned interventions in the organization's 'processes,' using behavioral-science knowledge."

Paradigm – A constellation of concepts, values, perceptions, and practices shared by a community which form a particular vision of reality and collective mood that is the basis of the way that the community organizes itself.

Pascale, Richard – Born in 1938, Richard Pascale was a member of the faculty of Stanford's Graduate School of Business for 20 years. Now a leading business consultant, he has written or co-authored three highly challenging books – *The Art of Japanese Management* (1981),[8] *Managing on the Edge* (1990),[9] and *Surfing the Edge of Chaos* (2000).[10]

Person Culture – One of four basic cultural types that operate to a greater or lesser extent in organizations. In this culture, the individual is the central point; there is no super-ordinate objective. Such structure as exists is only there to serve the individuals within it. The individuals are likely to have very strong values about how they should work.

Peters, Tom – Former McKinsey consultant and co-author (with Bob Waterman) of *In Search of Excellence*,[11] the most popular management book of recent times, with sales of over six million globally.

Power Culture – One of four basic cultural types, this model is like a web with a ruling spider. Those in the web are dependent on a central power source. There may be a specialist or functional structure but central control is exercised largely through appointing loyal key individuals and interventionist behavior from the center. For people working there, it can be a case of "Conform or Go!"

PYMWYMIC – A company that acts according to its values and beliefs, as in a Put Your Money Where Your Mouth Is Company.

Reality check - A reality check is any tool, technique, method, or device used by an individual or organization to provide feedback on their place in the world. Reality checks include tools and techniques that are recognized as "strategic" (such as industry analysis, competitor analysis, and so on) and many others that are not (customer research, employee feedback, or merely reading trade magazines).

Re-purposing - Originally coined by US TV executives to describe the process of "freshening up" a new series of a well-established TV series whose popularity is flagging by introducing new characters and plot-lines. The term is now being adopted by companies seeking to re-establish forward momentum.

Role Culture - One of four basic cultural types, a Role Culture is controlled by procedures, role descriptions, and clearly delegated authority. Co-ordination occurs at the top. Because it is a culture that values predictability and consistency, it is often slow to make changes.

Schein, Edgar - Born in 1928, and a Professor at the MIT Sloan School of Management, Edgar H. Schein is sometimes seen as the "inventor" of the idea of corporate culture. More recently, his work has explored the nature of the psychological contract between employer and employee, and also career anchors: the idea that we each have an underlying career value that we are unwilling to give up.

Scientific management - An approach to work devised around a century ago by Frederick Taylor that involved detailed observation and measurement of even the most routine work to find the optimum mode of performance. Taylor advocated the use of time-and-motion study as a means of analyzing and standardizing work activities.

Seven S model - Widely used analytical tool, devised by Richard Pascale and Anthony Athos, that evaluates organizations under seven key headings to which managers need to pay attention. The seven are: Strategy; Structure; Systems; Skills; Style; Shared values; and Staff. Some of these areas are "hard" (i.e. Strategy, Structure and Systems) and some are "soft" (Style, Staff and Shared values). "Skills" is placed center-stage because it is both "hard" and "soft," comprising both the distinctive capabilities of key personnel and the core competencies of the organization as a whole.

Shared vision – In a corporation, a shared vision changes people's relationship with the company. It is no longer "their company"; it becomes "our company." A shared vision is the first step in allowing people who mistrusted each other to begin to work together. It creates a common identity.

Strategic inflection points – A term coined by Andy Grove to describe a moment in the life of a business when its fundamentals are about to change for better or worse.

Subcultures – Very often, the culture in large organizations is not pervasive, singular, or uniform. In these organizations, there is not one single culture but a collection of subcultures. Subcultures may share certain characteristics, norms, values, and beliefs or be totally different. These subcultures can function co-operatively or be in conflict with each other.

Task Culture – One of four basic cultural types, a Task Culture exists in an organization where co-operation between units is a necessary part of delivering a project. In Task Cultures, there is an emphasis on results and getting things done. Individuals are empowered with discretion and control over their work.

Taylor, Frederick W. – The world's first efficiency expert and "the father of scientific management." Taylor's work with car-making legend Henry Ford led directly to the mass production techniques that created 15 million Model Ts between 1910 and 1927, and that set the pattern for industrial working practice world-wide.

Ten X force – Term used by Intel CEO Andy Grove to describe a super-competitive force that threatens the future of a business.

Transformation – A one-time, discontinuous shift in financial performance, industry benchmarks (e.g. cycle time, quality, costs), or climate. An indicator of transformation is when employees say theirs is a different organization to the one it was five years ago.

Underlying assumptions – Basic assumptions that have become so taken for granted that people in the organization would find it inconceivable to base their behavior on anything else. For example, a company's deeply held belief that the customer should always be treated with respect would render it almost impossible that organizational employees would set out to deliberately rip off customers. These deeply held assumptions are rarely articulated and even more rarely are they questioned unless some form of organizational crisis forces their re-examination.

Virtual organization – An organizational form that consists of a loose (and often temporary) combination of technology, expertise, and networks.

Vision – A company's view of its future that is compelling and stretching, but that is also viewed as achievable. A corporate vision for the future has to be grounded in awareness. If not, it quickly becomes a wish-driven strategy meritorious in all respects except for the fact that it will never be achieved.

Weber, Max – Weber (1864–1920) was a German university professor who was the first person to describe organizations as having the qualities of a machine, a metaphor that persisted throughout the twentieth century. Weber is sometimes described, unfairly, as the father of bureaucracy.

NOTES

1 http://www.alliesconsulting.com/resources/articles/idinflcult.html
2 Hamel, G. & Prahalad, C.K. (1994) *Competing for the Future*. Harvard Business School Press, Boston.
3 Herzberg, F. (1959) *Motivation to Work*. John Wiley, New York.
4 Recently republished as Maslow, A. (1998) *Maslow on Management*. John Wiley & Sons, New York.
5 Dawkins, R. (1976) *The Selfish Gene*. Oxford University Press, Oxford.
6 Morgan, G. (1986) *Images of Organization*. Sage, Newbury Park, California.
7 Beckhard, R. (1978) *Organization Development: strategies and models*. Addison-Wesley, Reading, MA.
8 Pascale, R. & Athos, A.G. (1981) *The Art of Japanese Management*. Warner Books, New York.
9 Pascale, R. (1990) *Managing on the Edge*. Simon & Schuster, New York.
10 Pascale, R., Millemann, M. & Gioja, L. (2000) *Surfing the Edge of Chaos*. Crown Business, New York.
11 Peters, T. (1982) *In Search of Excellence: Lessons from America's Best-Run Companies*. Harper & Row, New York.

Resources

Countless words have been written – directly and indirectly – about organizational culture. This chapter identifies some of the best resources around, including:

- » books
- » articles
- » journals, magazines, and Websites

BOOKS: AN ANNOTATED BIBLIOGRAPHY

Badaracco, J. (1997) *Defining Moments*. Harvard Business School Press, Boston, MA

Defining Moments is a book about work and life choices and the critical points at which the two become one. It examines the conflicts that every manager faces and presents an unorthodox yet practical way for managers to think about and resolve them. Drawing on philosophy and literature, and built around three stories of real-life quandaries of increasing complexity that managers have faced as their careers have advanced, the book provides tangible examples, actionable steps, and a flexible framework that managers at all levels can use to make the choices that will shape not only their careers but their characters.

Blackmore, S. (1999) *The Meme Machine*. Oxford University Press, Oxford

First coined by Richard Dawkins when updating Darwin's theory of natural selection in his ground-breaking book *The Selfish Gene* (1976), a meme is an idea, behavior, or skill that can be transferred from one person to another by imitation. Memes are replicators and are all around us in our everyday lives, competing to get into our brains and minds. Examples include the way in which we copy ideas, inventions, songs, catch-phrases, and stories from one another. Once humans learned to receive, copy, and retransmit memes, the rest, according to Blackmore, is a foregone conclusion – we are the product of our memes just as we are the products of our genes, with memes, like genes, caring only for their own propagation.

Memetic competition shapes our minds and culture, just as natural selection has designed our bodies. But why should this matter to us and the organizations we work for? Well for a start, it explains why the sexual adventures of an errant senior manager would grip the corporate imagination more than the latest set of financial figures.

Susan Blackmore explores her subject with great panache. Some readers who like to explore both sides of an argument before making up their own minds may find her sure-footed advocacy a little over-powering, but for the rest of us *The Meme Machine* is a riveting and provocative read.

Bridges, W. (1992) *The Character of Organizations*. Davies-Black Publishing, Palo Alto, CA

Just as people have personalities, so Bridges believes that organizations have characters. Using examples from companies like McDonald's, Hewlett-Packard, GE, and so on, Bridges identifies 16 organizational character types using the framework of MBTI personality types and shows how these influence what goes on within an organization.

Cairncross, F. (2002) *The Company of the Future*. Profile Books, London

According to Cairncross, we've badly underestimated the power of the Internet to alter the way companies behave. She asserts that managers and their companies must embrace and exploit the very technologies that have upended their jobs and their businesses. They must learn to wed technological and human skills in ways that enable effective talent management and customer relationship building, fast and flexible decision-making, and open, credible communications among all partners.

Carlzon, J. (1989) *Moments of Truth*. Harper and Row, New York

A classic text on what it really means to be customer-driven by the former CEO of Scandinavian Airlines (SAS). It focuses on those critical moments when we or our organization are judged by our customers, those "moments of truth" when we or our reports either excel or flop.

Cohen, B. & Greenfield, J. (1998) *Ben & Jerry's Double-Dip*. Fireside, New York

In 1978, Ben Cohen and Jerry Greenfield decided to set up their own business, an ice cream parlor based in Burlington, Vermont. Twenty years later, when this book was written, they had a $160mn international company and most of us could wander into a local supermarket and readily find a tub of their premium quality ice cream. What makes their success unusual is the extent to which they built their company around strong social values and iconoclastic thinking. For example, when they needed money to build a new plant, they ignored the more conventional capital-raising routes and held a Vermont-only public stock offering, effectively putting ownership of the company into the hands of the residents of their home state.

This book is an entertaining and often humorous read that tells how they built a "values driven company" before the term was invented. The narrative is liberally sprinkled with anecdotes, quotes from staff, customers, and entrepreneurial chums, as well as chunks of conversations between Ben and Jerry themselves.

de Geus, A. (1997) *The Living Company*. Nicholas Brealey, London

Drawing on unpublished research conducted by Shell in the early 1980s, Arie de Geus – the man widely credited for originating the concept of the "learning organization" – believes that most companies fail because they focus too narrowly on financial performance and pay insufficient attention to themselves as communities of human beings with the potential to learn, adapt, and grow. The living company, he says, emphasizes knowledge rather than capital, and adaptability rather than core competencies. De Geus won the Edwin G. Booz prize for Most Insightful Management Book back in 1997 and so it is a little disappointing that his ideas have not yet broken through into the mainstream. Nonetheless, anybody with an interest in organizational learning will find something of value here.

Donnellon, A. (1996) *Team Talk*. Harvard Business School Press, Boston, MA

Subtitled "The Power of Language in Team Dynamics," *Team Talk* uses anthropological and linguistic research techniques to focus on talk as the "medium through which team work is done and through which organizational and individual forces can be observed and analyzed." Given that language exchange is the primary way in which people swap information, make decisions and formulate plans, Donnellon's book represents the long overdue entry of sociolinguistics into the field of management studies.

Fineman, S. (1993) *Emotion in Organizations*. Sage, London

The ground-breaking book brings together a number of contributions from leading academics about how people can behave in companies and why this should be so. Not the easiest of reads, but it does make the point powerfully that a person's behavior always appears logical to that individual, no matter how irrational it might appear to others.

Gladwell, M. (2000) *The Tipping Point*. Little Brown, New York

Why do some minority tastes remain strictly minority, while others extend into the mainstream? *The Tipping Point* is a well written and racy exploration of what lies behind the point when a small fad acquires critical mass and takes off. It's very readable but the central idea isn't really enough to sustain a whole book – no surprise then to discover that it began its life as a long article in New Yorker magazine.

Hall, E.T. & Hall, M.R. (1987) *Hidden Differences: Doing Business With the Japanese*. Anchor Books/Doubleday, New York

A fascinating analysis and explanation of the unstated rules of Japanese–American business relations.

Handy, C. (2001) *The Elephant and the Flea*. Hutchinson, London

In his latest book (and his best for some time), self-styled social philosopher Handy explores the business world of the twenty-first century, which he claims "will be a world of fleas and elephants, of large conglomerates and small individual entities, of large political and economic blocs and small countries." The smart thing, it seems, is to be the flea on the back of the elephant because a flea can be global as easily as one of the elephants but can more easily be swept away. Elephants are a guarantee of continuity but fleas provide the innovation. A fascinating premise, outlined lucidly by Handy in one of the first "must-reads" of this century.

Hofstede, G. (1991) *Cultures and Organizations: Software of the Mind*. McGraw-Hill, London

Despite having separate and conflicting interests, nations and groups are faced with problems which require co-operation if they are to be solved. This book examines the differences in the way strategists think, and offers suggestions on how conflicts between them can be resolved.

Jaques, E. (1996) *Requisite Organization*. Cason Hall, Gloucester, MA

Based on Jaques' latest research, this is a thorough revision of the original book published in 1989. *Requisite Organization* challenges many current assumptions about effective organizations, particularly in the field of hierarchy – of which Jaques is a fan. Some may find his theories indigestible, but for those who persist there is a wealth of challenging material that undermines much conventional organizational wisdom.

Katzenbach, J. and Smith, D. (1993) *The Wisdom of Teams*. Harvard Business School Press, Boston, MA

According to Katzenbach and Smith – two senior McKinsey consultants – teams are "the primary building blocks of company performance." For this book, the authors talked with hundreds of people in more than 50 teams from 30 companies in a bid to discover what differentiates various levels of team performance, where and how teams work best, and how generally to enhance team effectiveness. Some of their findings are common sense – e.g. teams with a genuine commitment to performance goals and to a common purpose outperform those who place a greater emphasis on teambuilding. Others are at face value surprising (formal hierarchy, they say, is actually good for teams). In a chapter towards the end of the book they describe how top management can usefully support the development of a team-based culture.

Law, A. (1998) *Open Minds*. Orion, London

St Luke's is a high-profile London-based advertising agency and Andy Law has been the company's iconoclastic chairman since 1995. Owned entirely by its employees, all physical resources – offices, PCs etc. – in the company are shared, and there is little hierarchy. Employees are involved in almost all decisions, including setting their own pay rises. Whether the model developed at St Luke's has the resilience to cope with a downturn in its business fortunes (the company has enjoyed continuous growth since its creation) remains to be seen. In the meantime, *Open Minds* makes a compelling case study, describing and explaining as it does the business practices and philosophy behind this fascinating company.

Lewis, J. (1999) *Trusted Partners*. Free Press, New York

Mergers and alliances on an ever grander scale are a feature of the global economy. *Trusted Partners* describes how to build trust between organizations that are forging alliances of various types with other companies, and explores how interpersonal relationships are a critical element of that. Drawing on experience built over four decades of working with some of the world's leading companies, Lewis goes well beyond theoretical analysis of the nature of trust between corporate "rivals" to lay out some practical and eminently sensible steps involved in building and maintaining trust.

Maslow, A. (1998) *Maslow on Management*. John Wiley and Sons, New York

Abraham Maslow remains one of the most widely known experts on human behavior and motivation. His psychological perspectives on management, such as the hierarchy of needs, are still studied today in business schools all over the world. Now, 37 years after its original publication, Maslow's most influential business book, *Eupsychian Management*, has been updated to include commentaries by some of today's management thinkers, who discuss the continuing relevance of his ideas. *Maslow on Management* is a stimulating but not always easy read that demonstrates clearly why Maslow was an unparalleled thinker and innovator in applying human behavior to the workplace.

Morgan, G. (1986) *Images of Organization*. Sage, Newbury Park, CA

Fascinating description of use of metaphors and creative approaches in organizational work. If you haven't come across it, read it. It will open up new windows for looking at the organizational world.

Neuhauser, P., Bender, R. & Stromberg, K.L. (2000) *Culture.com*. John Wiley & Sons, New York

Sub-titled "Building Corporate Culture in the Connected Workplace," *Culture.com* is a practical handbook that guides the readers through nine key characteristics of a dotcom culture. The authors use case studies and interviews from business, nonprofit, and government settings to illustrate these change strategies in action. For ongoing information on their research into the people and companies who are living through the transition to e-business, try their Website, which can be found at www.culturedotcom.com.

Ridderstråle, J. & Nordström, K. (2000) *Funky Business: Talent Makes Capital Dance*. Financial Times/Prentice Hall, London

On the face of it, a business book by two Swedish professors about how successful companies differ from their competitors doesn't sound like the most riveting of reads. But *Funky Business* is no dry theoretical tome; and authors Ridderstråle and Nordström are not your standard issue academics. Unless, that is, it's normal for Swedish business professors to shave their heads, wear leather trousers, describe themselves as funksters, and call their public appearances gigs rather than seminars. Funky management, for Nordström and Ridderstråle, means innovation, constant change, and – especially – reliance on people as the main source of "sustainable uniqueness." This book draws extensively from rigorously researched data but presents its findings with wit and intelligence reinforced with excellent examples.

Schein, E.H. (1992) *Organizational Culture and Leadership*. Jossey Bass, San Francisco, CA

Focusing on the complex business realities of the 1990s, this second edition updates the author's understanding of culture. It demonstrates the crucial role that leaders play in successfully applying the principles of culture to achieve their organization's goals and fulfil their missions.

Schwartz, P. & Gibb, B. (1999) *When Good Companies Do Bad Things*. John Wiley, Chichester

In *When Good Companies Do Bad Things*, the authors discuss business ethics at companies such as Nestlé, Texaco, Union Carbide, Nike, and Royal Dutch/Shell. They examine incidents involving each of these companies, and suggest alternative approaches to the actual damage control methods adopted by the organizations in question when they were faced with (often highly public) challenges to their reputations.

Senge, P. (1990) *The Fifth Discipline*. Currency/Doubleday, New York

Senge's book was one of the first to popularize the concept of the learning organization. His five core disciplines that underpin the building of a learning community are Personal Mastery, Mental Models (the filters through which we view the world), Shared Vision, Team Learning, and Systems Thinking. The last of these, which Senge terms the cornerstone discipline, is covered in 70 pages in a section that represents an excellent generalist introduction to the main concepts of systems thinking, a core skill in a globalized, networked economy.

Simmons, A. (1998) *Territorial Games*. Amacom, New York

Territorial Games is a fascinating exploration of organizational turf wars – why they occur and what we can do about them. Simmons identifies and describes ten different territorial games that are enacted within organizations. These include:

» *occupation*: marking territory; monopolizing resources, relationships, or information;
» *information manipulation*: withholding, covering up, or giving false information;
» *strategic non-compliance*: agreeing to take action with no intention of acting; and

» *shunning*: personally excluding an individual; influencing a group to treat another as an outsider.

Simmons then goes on to examine what can be done to end turf wars at work, and to suggest a set of strategies by which the impact of territorial games can be defused.

Thornbury, J. (2000) *Living Culture*. Random House Business Books, London

Jan Thornbury designed and led the global culture change process for KPMG, with the goal of attracting and keeping good people. This book provides a clear model of how culture works in an organization, and what must be done to change it.

Trompenaar, F. (1997) *Ride the Waves of Culture*. Nicholas Brealey, London

Revised second edition that includes new case histories and fresh research findings. The book uses country-by-country graphs, examples, and other comparisons to clearly illustrate how different cultures respond to different management approaches. It also provides case histories to show how managers have successfully anticipated and mediated difficult and potentially costly dilemmas, and shows how managers can prepare their organizations for the process of internationalization through specific points of intervention.

ADDITIONAL BIBLIOGRAPHY

Bridges, W. (1992) *The Character of Organizations*. Davies-Black Publishing, Palo Alto, CA.

Conner, D.R. (1993) *Managing at the Speed of Change*. Villard Books, New York.

Dell, M. (1999) *Direct from Dell*. HarperCollins Business, New York.

Dunkerley, M. (1996) *The Jobless Economy*. Polity Press, Cambridge.

Egan, G. (1994) *Working the Shadow Side: A Guide to Positive Behind-the-Scenes Management*. Jossey Bass, San Francisco, CA.

Hall, E.T. & Hall, M.R. (1987). *Hidden Differences: Doing Business With the Japanese*. Anchor Books/Doubleday, New York.

Handy, C. (1993) *Understanding Organizations*, 4th edn. Penguin, London.

Hofstede, G. (1991). *Cultures and Organizations, Software of the Mind*. McGraw-Hill Limited, London.

Johnson, G. & Scholes, K. (1999) *Exploring Corporate Strategy*. FT Prentice Hall, London.

Keirsey, D. & Bates, M. (1984). *Please Understand Me: Character & Temperament Types*. Prometheus Nemesis Book Company, Del Mar, CA.

Klein, N. (2000) *No Logo*. Flamingo, London.

Kotter, J. & Heskett, J. (1992). *Corporate Culture and Performance*. The Free Press, New York.

Myers, I.B. (1993). *Introduction to Type*, 5th edn, revised by L.K. Kirby & K.D. Myers. Consulting Psychologists Press, Inc., Palo Alto, CA.

Negroponte, N. (1995) *Being Digital*. Knopf, New York.

Noer, D.M. (1993). *Healing the Wounds: Overcoming the Trauma of Layoffs and Revitalizing Downsized Organizations*. Jossey Bass Publishers, San Francisco, CA.

Schneider, B. (1987). ''The People Make the Place.'' *Personnel Psychology,* **40**, 450.

Schneider, W.E. (1994) *The Reengineering Alternative: A Plan for Making Your Current Culture Work*. Irwin Professional Publishing, New York.

Stacey, R. (1993) *Managing the Unknowable*. Jossey Bass, San Francisco, CA.

Tapscott, D., Ticoll, D. & Lowy, A. (2000) *Digital Capital*. Nicholas Brealey, Naperville.

ARTICLES (MOST RECENT FIRST)

''Good to Great.'' (2001) *Fast Company*, October.

Start with 1435 good companies. Examine their performance over 40 years. Find the 11 companies that became great. Now, here's how you can do it too.

"Can C.K. Prahalad Pass the Test?" (2001) *Fast Company*, August.

Can C.K. build a company around the principles that he has been teaching other high-powered leaders?

Bonabeau, E. & Meyer, C. (2001) "Swarm Intelligence: A Whole New Way to Think About Business." *Harvard Business Review,* May.
Webber, A.M. (2001) "How Business Is a Lot Like Life." *Fast Company*, April.

If you want your company to stay alive, then try running it like a living organism. The first rule of life is also the first rule of business: adapt or die.

Fulmer, R.M., Gibbs, P.A. & Goldsmith, M. (2000) "Developing Leaders: How Winning Companies Keep On Winning." *Sloan Management Review*, Fall.
Mintzberg, H. and Van der Heyden, L. (1999) "Organigraphs: Drawing How Companies Really Work." Harvard Business Review, September/October.
Nicholson, N. (1998) "How Hardwired is Human Behavior?" *Harvard Business Review,* July/August.

Evolutionary psychology asserts that human beings today retain the mentality of our Stone Age ancestors. We are, in other words, "hard wired" for certain attitudes and behaviors. If that is so, what are the implications for managers?

Schein, E.H. (1997) "Culture Matters." *Demos Quarterly*, **8**.
"Of soloists and session men." (1997) *The Economist*, February 22.

An exploration of the balance between individuality and fraternity among jazz musicians.

Collins, J.C. & Porras, J.I. (1996) "Building Your Company's Vision." *Harvard Business Review,* September/October.
Lipton, M. (1996) "Demystifying the development of an organizational vision." *Sloan Management Review*, Summer.

Although few would deny that vision serves a critical role in today's organizations, many managers can be intimidated and frustrated by the challenge of developing one. Mark Lipton explores vision by explaining how and why visions work (and why they sometimes fail). He goes on to present a template that outlines the principal themes necessary for an effective vision.

Schein, E.H. (1996) "Culture: The Missing Concept in Organization Studies." *Administrative Science Quarterly,* June.

According to Schein, lack of attention to social systems in organizations has led some researchers to underestimate the importance of culture in how organizations function. Concepts for understanding culture in organizations, says Schein, only have value when they derive from observation of real behavior in organizations, when they make sense of organizational data, and when they are definable enough to generate further study.

Kotter, J.P. (1995) "Leading Change: Why Transformation Efforts Fail." *Harvard Business Review,* March/April.

"The Vision Thing." (1994) *The Economist*, September.

Stayer, R. (1990) "How I learned to let my workers lead." *Harvard Business Review.* November/December.

This *Harvard Business Review* article tells the story of Ralph Stayer, who in the 1980s owned a successful, growing sausage company that had him badly worried. Commitment was poor, motivation was lousy, the gap between performance and potential was enormous. Over the next five years, Stayer turned the company upside down, but only by turning himself upside down first.

JOURNALS, MAGAZINES, AND WEBSITES

For readers wanting to keep up to date with developments in the strategy field, the following publications and Websites are worth dipping into on a regular basis.

Center for Business Innovation

Site managed by consultants Ernst and Young – quality of content varies but occasionally provokes thought.

» www.businessinnovation.ey.com

Company information

More and more companies are creating Websites, and the amount of information on them varies enormously, but many carry details of a company's vision, mission, values and the like. In the first instance, for UK companies, try www.companyname.co.uk; for US companies, try www.companyname.com.

The Economist

The best single source of information about what is happening in the world. A mainstream publication but one that will take on some big topics from time to time, and one whose take on the new economy is invariably insightful and clear-eyed.

» www.economist.com

Fast Company

The magazine is monthly and has been an essential read since it started up in 1996. Of late though, the content – whilst still excellent – has been swamped by increasing volumes of advertising. The companion Website is just about the best free site around on the future world of work (it also carries material not found in the magazine).

» www.fastcompany.com/home.html

Financial Times

Of all the dailies, *The Financial Times* provides the best in-depth coverage of organization-related issues.

» www.ft.com

Harvard Business Review

The most authoritative business monthly on the block. Has tended in the past to be more mainstream than truly ground-breaking in its coverage of business issues. That said, *HBR* has responded well to the challenge to traditional business thinking posed by the new economy, and recent issues have generally contained two or three relevant articles. Also, if you are interested in getting the lowdown on forthcoming books from Harvard's publishing wing several months before publication, the magazine consistently trails major books with articles from the authors. The Website provides overview of contents of the magazine – no free articles but the executive summaries are there and they are often all you need.

» www.hbsp.harvard.edu/home.html

Institute for Research on Intercultural Cooperation

An excellent starting point for anybody wanting to learn more about the work and thinking of Geert Hofstede.

» http://cwis.kub.nl/%7Efsw_2/iric/index2.htm

The Leadership & Organization Development Journal

The Leadership & Organization Development Journal aims to provide penetrating insights into the expected qualities of leaders in the current climate. It presents research and views on making and developing dynamic leaders, how organizations can and will change and how leaders can effect this. Contains some excellent links to free articles and information.

» www.emeraldinsight.com/lodj.htm

Management Link

A one-stop shop containing links to more than 100 key management Websites.

» www.inst.mgt.org.uk/external/mgt-link

People Management

The online magazine of the Chartered Institute of Personnel and Development.

» www.peoplemanagement.co.uk

Sloan Management Review

Since its founding in 1959, MIT's *Sloan Management Review* has covered all management disciplines, although its particular emphasis these days is on corporate strategy, leadership, and management of technology and innovation. Over the years it has featured articles by the likes of Peter Senge, Lester Thurow, James Brian Quinn, Gary Hamel, Thomas Davenport, Christopher Bartlett, Sumantra Ghoshal, John Quelch, Henry Mintzberg, Max Bazerman, and Ed Lawler.

» http://mitsloan.mit.edu/

www.edschein.com

Site is dedicated to the life and work of Edgar Schein, widely acclaimed as one of the founders of the field of organizational psychology.

www.hrnetwork.co.uk

This Website contains some excellent material about team development. It describes seven characteristics, represented by the acronym PERFORM, that are necessary for a group to become a high-performing team. The characteristics are: Purpose and values; Empowerment; Relationships and communication; Flexibility: Optimal productivity; Recognition and appreciation; and Morale.

www.imaginiz.com

Site dedicated to the work and thinking of Gareth Morgan.

Ten Steps to Managing Cultural Issues Effectively

- » Changing an organization's culture is messy, complicated business.
- » Ten factors that are key to managing cultural issues effectively
- » Key learning points

"Culture is one of the most precious things a company has, so you must work harder on it than anything else."

Herb Kelleher, CEO Southwest Airlines

What can a company do if current cultural assumptions are dysfunctional or out of alignment with environmental realities?

These days, the typical response is a "slash and burn" approach aimed at all those people and practices most closely associated with the old "failed" culture. Out goes the old leader and in comes a new managing director whose first act is to fire the top echelons of management and bring in his or her own people. The new leadership team then espouses a new set of values that match the business realities as they perceive them.

However, leaders who simply advocate a new way of thinking about customer delight, or team-based working, or empowerment, or complexity theory, or whatever, may talk in terms of "culture change," but they will not influence the existing culture one jot by this method. As Schein puts it:

"If the existing culture of the organization does not already value what the new 'right' way is supposed to be, the leader's words will fall on deaf ears. Even if the leader enlists an army of change agents to 'change the culture,' it is unlikely that they will get anywhere because people will not give up ways of thinking that they have come to take for granted, that are mostly tacit, and that have been the basis of the organization's prior success."[1]

There are more constructive approaches that an organization can put in place. In developing the following ten factors for managing cultural issues effectively, the assumption is that the current organizational status quo is unsatisfactory in some form or fashion. If all is hunkydory, then the clear message with culture is "Don't meddle – if it ain't broke, don't fix it."

The following ten factors, then, represent some distilled guidance on managing issues that have a cultural resonance. They are:

1 The crucial role of leadership.
2 Begin by focusing on the business problem.

3 Know who you are.

4 Undertake a cultural diagnosis.

5 Focus on those cultural elements that will help you get to where you need to go.

6 Identify the culture carriers who see the new direction and feel comfortable moving in that direction.

7 Build change teams around the new culture carriers.

8 Adjust the reward, incentive, and control systems to be aligned with the new desired strategy.

9 Take regular soundings.

10 Managing organizational culture against a backdrop of downsizing.

1. THE CRUCIAL ROLE OF LEADERSHIP

"The person who figures out how to harness the collective genius of the people in his or her organization is going to blow the competition away."

Walt Wriston, banker and writer

The best leaders know that their company's success hangs on how effectively they motivate and unleash the potential of others. They understand the Pygmalion Effect, namely that people behave the way they are treated: expect your team to fail and – sure enough – that's what will happen; treat them as competent, talented individuals and they'll live up to your expectations.

They also intuitively understand Buckminster Fuller's axiom that you never change things by fighting the existing reality; what you have to do is build a new model that makes the existing model obsolete. In a world of work where the rules of the game are being re-shaped before our eyes, their ability to put their own stamp on things enables them to become masters of, and not victims of, circumstance.

Edgar Schein has a lot to say about leadership and culture. He believes that the key issue for leaders is that they must become marginal in their own culture to a sufficient degree to recognize what may be its maladaptive assumptions. They must then learn some new ways of thinking themselves as a prelude to unfreezing and changing their organization. As Schein puts it: "This ability to perceive the limitations of one's own culture and to develop the culture adaptively is the essence and ultimate challenge of leadership.''

To leaders who fail to rise to this challenge, Schein gives this stark warning: ''The bottom line for leaders is that if they do not become conscious of the cultures in which they are embedded, those cultures will manage them. Cultural understanding is desirable for all of us, but it is essential to leaders if they are to lead.''

This is particularly pertinent if a group's survival is threatened because elements of its culture have become maladapted. In this situation, it is ultimately the function of leadership to recognize and do something about the situation.

2. START BY FOCUSING ON THE BUSINESS PROBLEM, AND THEN FIGURE OUT WHAT NEEDS TO BE DONE STRATEGICALLY AND TACTICALLY TO SOLVE IT

Before seeking to address any cultural issues, an organization needs to understand its mission or its primary task and ask itself whether it is being fulfilled. At this point, the issue is not culture at all; rather, it is about the organization's reason for continuing to exist.

Once this sense of purpose is embedded, the next vital step is to work out what the organization needs to do concretely in order to get where it wishes to go. Again, at this stage, it is not enough to simply say that the company needs a new culture. The new culture will flow from addressing real business needs effectively; corporate culture is a reflection of the company, not a solid entity that can be addressed and managed in its own right.

3. KNOW WHO YOU ARE

Sarah is a highly talented and creative marketing professional. She was headhunted from her previous position in that rarest of work environments – a successful dotcom – and was offered a significant hike in her salary to join a well-established life assurance company. She is just leaving her manager's office, having been told that her idea for a marketing campaign was brilliant but "far too racy for a company like us." On her way out, her boss adds that he appreciates the long hours she puts in but that he would nonetheless like to see her arriving in the office by 8:30am, the same time as everybody else. "Why on earth did I ever join this company?" she mutters to herself on her way back to her work cubicle.

When we are a member of a company with whom our personal outlook, values, and work ethos do not resonate, organizational culture becomes very visible and apparent to us. Like Sarah, we might feel entirely justified in ruing the day we joined this culturally hostile work environment.

The simple fact is that organizations are not all the same. They come in many shapes and sizes. Some are fast-moving, some make decisions at the pace of a lethargic snail on Prozac. Some depend on empowered individuals to meet corporate objectives, others prefer the command-and-control approach. For some, innovation is their lifeblood, for others the emphasis is on proven, reliable, trusted work practices.

As we have seen earlier, each of these organizational forms and approaches has come about on the back of an organization's earlier success. For some companies, the successful model has been the classical bureaucracy – the organization carefully sub-divided into functional departments, run from the top by the managing director and operating on a day-to-day basis by deploying an array of rules, regulations, job descriptions, and controls. The classical bureaucracy is designed to work like a machine, and generally it does indeed operate very efficiently – just as long as nothing changes!

For other companies, the model is more team-based, more like a fluid network of interaction than a bureaucratic structure. These companies encourage their people to exchange ideas and information. There is an open, evolving, learning-oriented approach to business. The organization is constantly on the look-out for new ideas, new systems, and new ways of working that will contribute to its success. This type of company is sometimes known as an adhocracy, an organization that evolves its form as it goes along.

There are plenty of other organizational forms we could explore, but the key point here is that organizational forms do not evolve by accident. Nor is there one best organizational form that every type of organization should aspire to.

4. UNDERTAKE A CULTURAL DIAGNOSIS

There is a well-known aphorism that if you want to find out about water, then you don't ask a fish. Just as water quickly becomes unremarkable to a fish, so an organization's culture can often become largely invisible to the people who have worked there for any length of time. If you have worked in the same place for more than one to two years, try tracking down somebody who has joined your company recently, say within the last three to four weeks, and ask them what they have particularly noticed, or what has struck them as unusual about the way things are done in your company.

Cultural diagnosis is a vital part of the change process because it allows us to become aware of the filters that we use to process our experience, both as individuals and as members of organizations, and the degree of "selectivity" that is involved in interpreting those experiences. It is a complex area, not least because it deals directly with the foibles that we have as human beings.

One useful concept is that of the "cultural web" in which the organization is understood in terms of the routines, rituals, stories, structures, and systems that exist within it. It can be used to elicit the organizational paradigm because each component of the cultural web provides clues about taken-for-granted organizational assumptions.

THE CULTURAL WEB – CULTURE IN THREE LAYERS[2]

Although an organization often espouses its values publicly (in mission and belief statements), diagnosing organizational culture is far more difficult in practice. Edgar Schein argues that organizational culture can be seen as consisting of three layers.

1 *Values*: These are often written down and discussible but tend to be expressed in vague terms such as "service to the community" or "equal opportunities."
2 *Beliefs*: These are more specific but again are issues that people can surface and talk about (such as a belief that the company should not trade with Iran).
3 *Taken-for-granted assumptions*: These are the real core of the organization's culture; aspects of the organizational life which people find difficult to identify and explain, and are known as the organizational *paradigm*.

Analyzing the cultural web of an organization is a long and complex process. Normally, it is done through the use of questions. By looking at the aspects of assumptions that "show through" in company stories and folklore, we can deduce what lies hidden "below the waterline." For example, a simple and effective way of gathering clues through organizational stories is to ask people to describe "the most significant things that have happened to the company in the last two to three years." Observing which stories people *select* is an important clue to the taken-for-granted assumptions. Some of the questions frequently asked are shown in the questionnaire in the box that follows.

SOME USEFUL QUESTIONS FOR ANALYZING THE CULTURE OF AN ORGANIZATION[3]
Stories
» What core beliefs do stories reflect?
» How pervasive are these beliefs (through levels)?
» Do stories relate to:
  » Strengths and weaknesses?
  » Successes or failures?
  » Conformity or mavericks?

» Who are the villains and heroes?

» What norms do the mavericks deviate from?

Routines and rituals

» Which routines are emphasized?

» What would look odd if changed?

» What behavior do routines encourage?

» What are the key rituals?

» What core beliefs do they reflect?

» What do training programs emphasize?

» How easy are rituals/routines to change?

Organizational structure

» How mechanistic/organic are the structures?

» How flat/hierarchical are the structures?

» How formal/informal are the structures?

» Do the structures encourage collaboration or competition?

» What type of power structure do they support?

Control systems

» What is most closely monitored/controlled?

» Is the emphasis on reward or punishment?

» Are controls related to history or current strategies?

» Are there many/few controls?

Power structures

» What are the core beliefs of the leadership?

» How strongly held are these beliefs (idealists or pragmatists)?

» How is power distributed in the organization?

» What are the main blockages to change?

Symbols

» What language and jargon is used?

» How internal or accessible is it?

» What aspects of strategy are highlighted in publicity?

» What status symbols are there?

» Are there particular symbols which denote the organization?

Overall

» What is the dominant culture (defender, prospector, analyzer)?

» How easy is it to change?

We need not take the matter any further here; except to note the importance for organizations in acknowledging the "rules of the game" that are actually in use. These are as likely to be invisible and covert as they are to be visible and overt. There are no short cuts here; understanding organizational culture is a long-term process, which can only be driven by a personal commitment to change.

When there is clear consensus on what needs to be done, examine the existing culture to find out how present tacit assumptions would aid or hinder what needs to be done. Not all the parts of a given culture are relevant to any given problem. Therefore general cultural analyses can be a major waste of time. Only when you know where you want to go, does it become relevant to ask how the culture will aid or hinder you.

5. FOCUS ON THOSE CULTURAL ELEMENTS THAT WILL HELP YOU GET TO WHERE YOU NEED TO GO

It is generally far easier to build up the strengths of the culture than to change those elements that are dysfunctional or weak. According to Edgar Schein,[4] culture is all too often seen only as a constraint. In reality, the strong elements of the culture and the diversity that may exist within the organization's various subcultures will almost certainly provide opportunities for building on existing strengths. This is a far more productive approach than risking getting bogged down with overcoming constraints.

6. IDENTIFY THE CULTURE CARRIERS WHO SEE THE NEW DIRECTION AND FEEL COMFORTABLE MOVING IN THAT DIRECTION

"This ability to perceive the limitations of one's own culture and to develop the culture adaptively is the essence and ultimate challenge of leadership."

Edgar Schein[5]

Even the most charismatic and visionary of business leaders cannot change organizations on their own. Successful change depends on bringing people along with you: in other words, aligning the personal vision of individuals to the wider vision of the organization itself. This isn't just about gaining the grudging acceptance of organizational reality by employees; it requires a deep sense of emotional commitment on the part of leaders and employees alike to making change happen. For this to occur, individuals must see the shared vision as an extension of their personal vision rather than a series of sacrifices to their personal interests.

Peter Senge, Director for the Center of Organizational Learning at MIT's Sloan School of Management, talks of the process as lining up all the arrows, making sure that the energy of individuals is flowing in the same direction so that it complements itself and contributes to the overall vision of the organization. In this sense, alignment is all about freeing the flow, so that individual energies can be liberated in the service of a common objective:

> In a corporation, a shared vision changes people's relationship with the company. It is no longer "their company"; it becomes "our company." A shared vision is the first step in allowing people who mistrusted each other to begin to work together. It creates a common identity.[6]

Alignment is an exceptionally difficult concept to grasp because few of us have direct experience of it in real life. What experience we have is normally found outside of our working life; playing team sports, playing music in a band, as part of a charitable group, or where we work with like-minded individuals engaged in our favorite hobby or pastime. It is something we experience in a "feeling sense" that generates excitement, passion, and a sense of "whole-ness." These are times when we feel that it is a pleasure to be alive. It is often marked by a lack of awareness of the passing of time; we "wake up" shocked that a whole day has somehow passed.

Transferring this alignment to an organizational setting is far more challenging. Building a shared sense of vision is predicated on a number of factors: the ability of a leader to crystallize the vision;

the presence of a safe and trusting environment within which individual creativity can flourish; and the willingness of individuals to take personal responsibility for achieving the organizational vision, either on their own, or as part of a wider team. However, when shared vision is genuinely achieved, the effect on an organization can be dramatic.

Empowering the specific employees and managers whose assumptions are already in line with the new strategy that is needed is a necessary first step to create role models to show others what the new direction of thinking and acting might be. These "culture leaders" are often found in more marginal managerial roles or in subcultures that have developed in the organization.

7. BUILD CHANGE TEAMS AROUND THE NEW CULTURE CARRIERS

The next stage of the process is for the leader of the change to put in place a change team or (more likely) a number of change teams. Each change team will have to diagnose the situation in the part of the organization which functions in its own area. The team will have to assume that different groups and different individuals will have to be treated differently to produce the changes in thinking and acting that are desired.

Opportunities for individuals to shape organizational culture are increased by the fact that certain personality types tend to cluster into disciplines and fields of employment. For example, a higher than average number of extroverts work in fields like marketing, public relations, and acting; while a disproportionate number of introverts are found in the fields of engineering, library work, and computer programming. Similarly, a disproportionate number of police detectives and farmers are sensing types who rely on step-by-step application of logic, while many writers, social scientists, and research assistants are intuitive types. The net result is that many organizations are inhabited by a non-random population of individuals with similar preferences. This homogeneity provides increased impetus and decreased resistance to the shaping of a desirable culture.

8. ADJUST THE REWARD, INCENTIVE, AND CONTROL SYSTEMS TO BE ALIGNED WITH THE NEW DESIRED STRATEGY

"Every group must know what its heroic and sinful behaviors are and must achieve consensus on what is a reward and what is a punishment."

Edgar Schein[7]

A company's reward and other systems must reinforce the desired new directions. This, according to Schein, is a step that is often overlooked. For example, management announces the need for teamwork but all the pay and incentive systems continue to be based on individual performance and individuals are competitively compared with each other when deciding upon promotions and bonuses.

In the same way, the company should aim to bring the structures and routine processes of the organization into alignment with the desired new direction. For example, it is important to use recruitment and selection methods that will control who is added to each department or office. Through this process of job matching, every new appointment made by the organization sends a message about the type of person who will thrive in the new environment.

Just as selection systems – not to mention reward, incentive, and control systems – must be consistent with the desired new direction, so the basic organization design must also facilitate what the new strategy demands. For example, if the new strategy requires teamwork across functional or product groupings it is important to weaken the power of the functional and business unit managers and strengthen the power of the project managers. The performance review system should focus attention on the new behaviors expected of organizational members; likewise, training programs should explicitly promote the new behavior sets.

9. TAKE REGULAR SOUNDINGS

Addressing cultural issues is not a one-off exercise. Although culture is perhaps the most stable element in organizations (because it is the product and residue of past success), the most positive and productive of cultures can rapidly degenerate. Companies like Marconi have shown just how swift can be a corporate fall from grace.

For this reason, organizational leaders need to pay ongoing attention to their company's culture. They should be continually asking themselves what the impact of their personal behavior and their business decisions might be on the business.

Here are a selection of the questions all leaders should regularly address about the state of their organizational culture.

» Do you understand the current mood within your organization?
» Are the strategic objectives of the company and the culture currently in alignment?
» What aspects of the culture need to change over the coming months?
» What is the ideal culture, and what is the gap between the ideal and the "real" culture?
» Are my actions consistent with the kind of organization I want this company to be?
» What are the key cultural leverage points for organizational change?
» What are the key elements of culture that function as the glue that holds the organization together?
» Are there any cultural misalignments that have emerged from recent structural changes in the business?
» How do key members of the management team fit with the culture I'm trying to create?
» What does our track record in attracting and retaining employees tell me about how people view the company?
» How many people in this company are familiar with the published vision and mission statement?
» How strong is the current culture?
» What new behaviors are necessary to help the company succeed in the future?

10. MANAGING ORGANIZATIONAL CULTURE AGAINST A BACKDROP OF DOWNSIZING

There are five particularly significant implications for the corporate culture when a company embarks on a downsizing exercise:[8]

1 The balance of power – if it was ever there in the first place – shifts explicitly from rank-and-file employees in the direction of top management. It is a top management decision who has a future within the organization and who does not. All too often, the underlying message is: "If you want to continue to work here, you will have to work harder and longer, be more responsive, be more of a team player etc."

2 Accompanying this power shift is a re-directing of focus away from the well-being of individuals to whatever steps are required to secure the well-being of the organization.

3 Basic assumptions about working relationships are likely to change, shifting from being "familial" to being more divisive and more competitive.

4 The employer–employee relationship is no longer assumed to be long-term and stable; rather its focus has become short-term and contingent.

5 Both employers and surviving employees have cause to revisit the value of concepts like commitment and loyalty.

Downsizing can either reinforce or destabilize organizational culture. It is possible to distinguish which downsizing practices tend to reinforce (or leave alone) existing culture from those which destabilize – intentionally or unintentionally – the current culture, as Table 10.1 demonstrates.[9]

In the final analysis, it is the cultural mindset of the managing director that will determine whether and how downsizing is implemented in an organization.

Addressing all of these elements thoroughly and professionally takes a great deal of time and energy on the part of all involved. But the key to making successful change comes from the base point of seeing a clear solution to a clear business problem. Ungrounded platitudes about new cultures or new values achieve nothing.

To give the last word on the subject to Edgar Schein:

"If culture change occurs, it does so as a by-product of fixing the fundamental problems that the organization's leaders identify and the new strategies upon which they embark. For this reason there is no such thing as a prescribed "right" culture for an organization,

Table 10.1   Cultural reinforcers and destabilizers..

Culture reinforcing	Culture destabilizing
Voluntary reductions (e.g. attrition, buyouts, job sharing)	Involuntary reductions (layoffs)
Advance notice given	Sudden termination without notice
Shared pain (e.g. cuts across all levels)	Winners/losers (e.g. executives get big bonuses while others lose their jobs)
Explicit criteria exist to determine "who stays, who goes"	Criteria are veiled in secrecy
Outplacement support provided for those who depart	No assistance provided to departing employees
"Survivors" given support to help them deal effectively with corporate life post-downsizing	Little or no assistance given.
Participation in direction-setting from various levels in organization	Goal setting done at top without input

only a right strategy within the limits of the culture that the organization already has. And ... if the present culture really prevents correcting the business strategy in some fundamental way, that culture will be broken up by destroying the group and eliminating the culture carriers, or the organization will fail and die.

Culture is perhaps the most stable element in organizations because it is the product and residue of past success. If we want our organizations to become more competitive and effective we would do well to take culture very seriously and stop bandying it about as if it were a suit of clothes to be changed at will."[10]

KEY LEARNING POINTS IN THIS CHAPTER

Ten factors that are key to managing cultural issues effectively.
1 The crucial role of leadership.
2 Begin by focusing on the business problem.
3 Know who you are.

4 Undertake a cultural diagnosis.
5 Focus on those cultural elements that will help you get to where you need to go.
6 Identify the culture carriers who see the new direction and feel comfortable moving in that direction.
7 Build change teams around the new culture carriers.
8 Adjust the reward, incentive, and control systems to be aligned with the new desired strategy.
9 Take regular soundings.
10 Managing organizational culture against a backdrop of downsizing.

NOTES

1 Schein, E.H. (1996) "Culture Matters." *Demos Quarterly*, **8**.
2 Adapted from Johnson, G. & Scholes, K. (1999) *Exploring Corporate Strategy*. FT Prentice Hall, London (itself adapted from Schein, E. (1992) *Organizational Culture and Leadership*. Jossey Bass, San Francisco).
3 Adapted from Johnson, G. & Scholes, K. (1999) *Exploring Corporate Strategy*. FT Prentice Hall, London.
4 Schein, E.H. (1997) "Culture Matters." *Demos Quarterly*, **8**.
5 Schein, E.H. (1992) *Organizational Culture and Leadership*. Jossey Bass, San Francisco.
6 Senge, P. (1990) *The Fifth Discipline*. Currency/Doubleday, New York.
7 Schein, E.H. (1992) *Organizational Culture and Leadership*. Jossey Bass, San Francisco.
8 Derived from an article by Thomas A. Hickok entitled "Downsizing and Organizational Culture." www.pamij.com/hickok.html
9 ibid.
10 Schein, E.H. (1997) "Culture Matters." *Demos Quarterly*, **8**.

Frequently Asked Questions (FAQs)

Q1: What is culture?

A: Many people – both theorists and practitioners – have offered their definitions of the term. The most widely used definition of culture is "the way we do things around here" but perhaps the most complete definition is by Edgar Schein, who describes it as ". . . a pattern of shared basic assumptions that the group learned as it solved its problems of external adaptation and internal integration, that has worked well enough to be considered valid and, therefore, to be taught to new members as the correct way to perceive, think, and feel in relation to those problems" (see Chapter 1).

Q2: How is culture formed in a new organization?

A: The building blocks of an organization's culture are the assumptions, values, and operating procedures of the founders, the qualities and characteristics of the people who join the organization, and the responses of the organization to events and challenges. In a young and growing organization, the personal behavior of the leader is by far the most important determinant of how the culture is shaped (see Chapter 10).

Q3: Are there different types of culture?

A: There are countless! Writer, management guru, and social philosopher Charles Handy has drawn on the work of Roger Harrison to suggest that there are four basic cultural types that operate to a greater or lesser extent in western organizations.

The four classifications are:

1 Power Cultures
2 Role Cultures
3 Task Cultures
4 Person Cultures.

For more information, see Chapter 6.

Q4: Who are the key figures in organizational culture theory?

A: They are literally too numerous to mention. Three who have been particularly influential over the past 20 years have been Edgar Schein, Gareth Morgan, and Geert Hofstede. More recently, Andy Law, Chairman at St Luke's advertising agency, has offered some interesting observations from a practitioner's perspective (see Chapter 2).

Q5: Is there such a thing as an ideal culture?

A: Absolutely not. There is no right or wrong culture, no better or worse culture, except in relation to what the organization is trying to do. A team of fire fighters will necessarily have a different set of operating patterns to an advertising agency.

Q6: My organization needs to change its culture – how can we make a start?

A: Start by focusing on the business problem, not the culture. Before trying to address any cultural issues, you'll need to understand your organization's mission or primary task. Then ask yourself whether it is being fulfilled. The next step is to work out what the organization needs to do concretely in order to get where it wishes to go. Again, at this stage, it is not enough to simply say that the company needs a new culture. The new culture will flow from addressing real business needs effectively; corporate culture is a reflection of the company, not a solid entity that can be addressed and managed in its own right.

Q7: What role does the leader of an organization play in the culture change process?

A: An absolutely critical role! The direction and focus that a good leader instills in an organization can create a real sense of organizational purpose. And through their behaviors and actions, leaders set the tone of an organization. The bottom line is that if leaders do not become conscious of the cultures in which they are embedded, those cultures will manage them. Cultural understanding is desirable for all of us, but it is essential to leaders if they are to lead effectively.

Q8: What are the drivers of culture change?

A: Most commonly, it is crisis not comfort that propels significant cultural change. When all is going well for a business, changing the formula is often the last thing on anybody's mind. An organizational crisis is often the spur to bringing in a new leader, somebody who can bring something different to the party. These new leaders, unhampered by past decisions, old loyalties, or corporate blind spots, are more likely to have the clarity of vision to realize that the corporate formula (and hence the corporate culture) needs to change radically. For an example of a company that successfully addressed a critical situation, see the case study on EDS in Chapter 7.

Q9: How valuable are case studies on organizations that have successfully changed their cultures?

A: Case studies very rarely produce solutions that can be transplanted wholesale in a different company. Nonetheless, they will always throw up questions and may often suggest a way forward. (see Chapter 7).

Q10: How can I find out more?

A: The problem is not accessing information about organizational culture – there are literally thousands of books and articles published every year. The trick is to distinguish the useful from the irrelevant or derivative. For some recommendations, see Chapter 9.

Index

Printed and bound in the UK by
CPI Antony Rowe, Eastbourne

Printed and bound by CPI Group (UK) Ltd, Croydon, CR0 4YY

13/04/2025

14656458-0002